Sensory Integration

A Guide for Preschool Teachers

Christy Isbell and Rebecca Isbell

P9-BYG-131

Dedication

This book is dedicated to our family. Their love and support has made this book and many other projects in our lives possible. Thank you.
—*Christy and Rebecca*

Acknowledgments

Special thanks to the preschool teachers of the East Tennessee State University Child Study Center and Little Buccaneers Student Childcare Center for their willingness to allow us to visit their classrooms and take photographs for this book.

Disclaimer

While this book concerns children with sensory integration disorders, the photographs used in the book do not necessarily include children with the specified disorder.

Special Thanks

We would like to thank some very special people who have worked diligently on the development of this book. Sheila P. Smith was the final person in the office to put her finishing touches on the words and organization of the content. Her questions and careful editing have made her an essential person on this project. Michael O. Talley has contributed the many fabulous photographs that are used in our book. These visuals will help you "see" what is being described in the text. Roxanne K. Stanley has been invaluable for the work she has done related to the many details that must be completed, including research, reviewing photographs, and photo releases. Rhonda Harper, OTR/L reviewed the text and provided us with guidance on terminology that would be useful for preschool teachers. Our thanks are given to these four highly competent individuals.

GH16561
A Gryphon House Book

Sensory Integration

A Guide for Preschool Teachers

Christy Isbell and Rebecca Isbell

Bulk purchase

Gryphon House books are available for special premiums and sales promotions as well as for fund-raising use. Special editions or book excerpts also can be created to specification. For details, contact the Director of Marketing at Gryphon House.

Disclaimer

Gryphon House, Inc. and the authors cannot be held responsible for damage, mishap, or injury incurred during the use of or because of activities in this book. Appropriate and reasonable caution and adult supervision of children involved in activities and corresponding to the age and capability of each child involved, is recommended at all times. Do not leave children unattended at any time. Observe safety and caution at all times.

Sensory Integration: A Practical Guide for Preschool Teachers

© 2007 Christy Isbell and Rebecca Isbell
Photographs by Michael Talley

Published by Gryphon House, Inc.
10726 Tucker Street, Beltsville, MD 20705
800.638.0928; 301.595.9500; 301.595.0051 (fax)

Visit us on the web at www.ghbooks.com

All rights reserved. No part of this publication may be reproduced, stored in a retrieval system, or transmitted in any form or by any means, electronic, mechanical, photocopying, recording or otherwise, without the prior written permission of the publisher. Printed in the United States of America. Every effort has been made to locate copyright and permission information.

Cover Art: Straight Shots Product Photography, Ellicott City, MD; www.get-it-shot.com.

Library of Congress Cataloging-in-Publication

Isbell, Christy.
  Sensory integration : a practical guide for preschool teachers / Christy Isbell and Rebecca Isbell ; photographs by Michael Talley
      p. cm.
  Includes bibliographical references and index.
  ISBN: 978-0-87659-060-7

  1. Children with disabilities--Education (Preschool) 2. Sensory disorders
in children. I. Isbell, Rebecca T. II. Title.
  LC4019.2.I82 2007
  371.9'0472--dc22

                                2007000885

Gryphon House is a member of the Green Press Initiative, a nonprofit program dedicated to supporting publishers in their efforts to reduce their use of fiber-sourced forests. This book is made of 30% post-consumer waste. For further information, visit www.greenpressinitiative.org.

Table of Contents

Chapter 3: Design the Environment to Support the Sensory Development of All Children 51

Chapter 4: Help for Preschoolers with Sensory Processing Disorder...75

Chapter 5: Practical Solutions to Meet the Needs of Individual Children During the Daily Routine 99

Chapter 6: Building and Creating Low-Cost Items 119

What Are Sensory Integration and Sensory Processing Disorder?

CHAPTER 1

Sensory Integration

Some children in your classroom may respond to their environment in ways that seem confusing or worrisome, and you may not be sure how to handle their behavior. Some unusual behaviors may be similar to these:

❖ Thomas covers his ears when the children are singing.
❖ Temple rolls all over the floor while others are sitting in circle time.
❖ Brianna refuses to touch playdough, sand, or paint.
❖ Miguel climbs on top of tables and jumps off.
❖ Cassandra often falls down and skins her knees.
❖ William refuses to play on outdoor playground equipment.

All of these children are demonstrating signs of problems with sensory integration (SI). So, how can you design or change your environment so that these children can learn and function effectively in the classroom?

Sensory integration is the neurological process of organizing sensory inputs for function in daily life.

This book explains why children with sensory integration problems behave differently in the preschool environment. "Red flags" in each chapter help identify children who have difficulties with sensory processing, also known as Sensory Processing Disorder (SPD), and simple, easy-to-use solutions are provided to address the sensory needs of young children in preschool. Many of the ideas offered will improve the environment for all children, not just those who have sensory processing problems.

Sensory integration is the neurological process of organizing sensory inputs for function in daily life. Our brains take in information from the body and interpret that information so that we can survive and make sense of our world. We use our senses to learn and develop. We also use our senses to help us interact appropriately within the environment.

We learn early about the five senses of touch, sight, hearing, taste, and smell. However, most of us are not aware of two additional senses that are just as important. Our sense of movement and balance (vestibular sense) interprets information through our inner ears to determine if our bodies are moving or standing still. Our vestibular sense tells our brains that our bodies are moving through space even while we are riding a rollercoaster through a completely dark indoor area where our vision cannot provide information. Our sense of body position (proprioceptive sense) provides our brains with information about our body parts and where they are in space. Proprioceptive awareness helps us determine where our heads, arms, and legs are located at any time, allowing us to walk up stairs without looking down at our feet.

Sensory integration occurs in the central nervous system (brain, spinal cord, and nerves). The process occurs automatically as the body gathers information through the skin, muscles, joints, inner ear, eyes, nose, and mouth. As you read this book, your brain works to integrate the many sensory inputs from your body. For example, you are reading the words on this page while you process other sensory information simultaneously: you might see the background view of the surrounding room; hear the sounds of an air conditioner, the television in the next room, and children talking; feel a blanket wrapped over your legs; taste the lemonade you are drinking; and smell a candle burning. You might also feel that you are sitting on the couch (vestibular) with your head up and your legs crossed (proprioceptive). The brain constantly focuses on sensory information—screening, organizing, and responding to input—so that the body can function. This is sensory integration (SI).

Development of Senses

Sensory processing begins in the womb and continues to develop throughout childhood. As a child's central nervous system matures, so does the child's sensory system. Infants can use their senses at a very young age, although the senses are not refined. Most people have fully functioning sensory systems by the time they reach adolescence.

A newborn infant's sensory skills are quite different from those of a preschooler. A newborn reacts to most types of touch with

protective responses. For instance, a newborn will withdraw his leg in response to a touch on the sole of his foot. By three years of age, he will learn to differentiate types of touch and will laugh when his foot is tickled or will pull his foot away from a toy that he steps on. A young infant can identify his mother by smell, but appears unaware of most other smells in the environment. Most preschoolers can identify common smells, such as muffins baking in the kitchen, and they can also tell you that muffins taste sweet.

Each of the seven senses develops at its own rate. Vision, hearing, movement, and body position sensations typically take more time to mature. A newborn infant lacks the ability to identify colors or shapes. By three years of age, many children can see objects at far distances and can tell the difference between shapes and colors. And although a newborn can hear, he is not capable of identifying a sound or its location. Most preschoolers can identify and localize distant sounds, such as their teacher's voice from across the playground.

Each child will develop sensory skills at his own pace. However, there is a wide range of "typical" sensory development and skills. Genetics and environmental influences play a role in sensory development. For instance, some children are more prone to ear infections because of the way their inner ears are formed (genetics). Other children are more likely to have ear infections because they live in environments where they are exposed to second-hand smoke. It is common for both of these influences to cause young children to have problems with the sense of hearing. All the senses need to work together so that preschoolers can reach their fullest potential. Preschoolers must be able to coordinate all seven senses to learn about their world and function effectively.

Background on Sensory Integration

A. Jean Ayres, Ph.D., was an occupational therapist and educational psychologist who researched sensory integration in the mid 1900s. Ayres identified the diagnosis of sensory integration dysfunction, developed Sensory Integration Theory, and, in 1973, published her groundbreaking book, *Sensory Integration and Learning Disorders.* Ayres designed assessment tools for sensory integration dysfunction and taught many occupational therapists how to assess and treat children with sensory integration dysfunction. Sensory Integration Theory remains the basis of assessment and intervention of children with sensory integration (SI) problems.

Many occupational therapists have continued the work that Ayres began, as health professionals, parents, and educators have become aware of the diagnosis and its treatment. Carol Kranowitz's (2006) book, *The Out-of-Sync Child: Recognizing and Coping with Sensory Processing Disorder, Revised Edition,* helped many people, including early childhood educators, to become more aware of how deficits in SI can impact young children's daily lives.

> **Sensory Processing Disorder (SPD) occurs when a person's brain does not organize sensory signals and he or she is unable to respond appropriately.**

What Is Sensory Processing Disorder?

Sensory Processing Disorder (SPD) is difficulty in using the information that is collected through the senses (vision, hearing, touch, taste, smell, movement, and body awareness) in daily life. Most people are born with the ability to take in sensory information, organize the information, and respond appropriately. For example, when you smell cookies burning in the oven, see smoke, and hear the oven timer buzzing, you go to the kitchen and remove the cookies from the oven. This is an appropriate response to the sensory information that the brain receives through your nose, eyes, and ears. SPD occurs when a person's brain does not organize those sensory signals and he is unable to respond effectively. Using the same example, if a person responded to the cookies burning by placing his hands over his ears and yelling, this would be a disorganized and ineffective response and would make it difficult for him to function effectively in his environment.

Categories of Sensory Processing Disorder

SPD is an all-inclusive term for a group of neurological disorders. There are three main categories of SPD: Sensory Modulation Disorder (SMD), Sensory Discrimination Disorder (SDD), and Sensory-Based Motor Disorder (SBMD) (see Figure 1).

Figure 1: Types of Sensory Processing Disorders

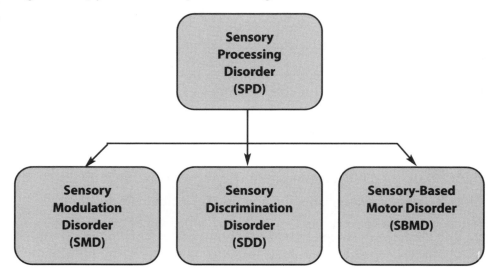

Miller, L. J., Cermak, S. A., Lane, S. J., Anzalone, M. E. & Koomar, J. A. (Summer 2004). Position statement on terminology related to Sensory integration dysfunction. *S.I. Focus* magazine.

Sensory Modulation Disorder (SMD) is the most common type of Sensory Processing Disorder (SPD), and the signs and symptoms are recognizable by many educators and parents. Preschoolers who have these types of sensory problems are most likely to make teachers and parents concerned. Preschoolers who have a Sensory Modulation Disorder (SMD) will often have difficulties in areas of development such as social-emotional skills, gross motor skills, fine motor skills, play skills and self-help skills. These children may also demonstrate behavior problems and show signs of low self-esteem secondary to their sensory disorders. Deficits in these areas of development can have a significant, negative impact on a preschooler's ability to learn and participate in preschool. Therefore, the focus of this book will be on young children who have SMD. Early childhood educators can use the information that follows to identify children who are in this category of SPD. Preschool teachers can also use this resource to help select and implement sensory-based methods that will allow young children to succeed in the learning environment.

For the purpose of this book, Sensory Discrimination Disorder (SDD), and Sensory-Based Motor Disorder (SBMD) will not be presented (see Figure 1). These two categories of Sensory Processing Disorder (SPD) are less common and very difficult for those without advanced training in sensory integration to identify. Assessment and intervention for children who fall into these two categories are typically designed and implemented by pediatric occupational therapists.

Responses to Sensory Input

Everyone experiences occasional sensory difficulties. Most people learn how to adjust and manage sensory input so their response to the input becomes "adaptive" and does not cause difficulty during daily activities. For example, someone who does not like the feeling of tags in the back of his shirts will simply cut the tags off of his clothing. Or, a person who gets carsick while riding on a winding road may choose to drive so that he can visually focus on the road. These are not examples of SPD; rather, they demonstrate isolated problems with sensory processing. These people have learned how to change or adjust to the situation so that they do not feel uncomfortable.

Our ability to understand sensory input and respond in a functional manner follows a developmental progression. For example, Caroline, a typically developing six-year-old, is over-sensitive to certain sounds in her environment. At bedtime, if the television is too loud in the next room, Caroline is unable to calm down enough to fall asleep. When she was two years old, Caroline would cry and whine if the TV was too loud. Now that she is six, Caroline has learned to simply ask her father to lower the volume and close her door before climbing into bed. This is an effective response to her inability to process the auditory input; she is not demonstrating SPD.

Many children are unable to produce an adaptive or effective response to some types of sensory input. Some children are easily over-stimulated by

Our ability to understand sensory input and respond in a functional manner follows a developmental progression.

certain sensory inputs and try to avoid them. Other children are on the opposite end of the spectrum. These children are under-stimulated by some sensory inputs. Some need stimulation but don't know how to get it. Others crave more input than the typical child. Children on either end of the spectrum have sensory processing problems that hinder their participation in learning and life activities.

Under-Stimulated ◄————Typical Response————► Over-Stimulated

Fisher is a three-year-old boy who seems to be in constant motion. While three-year-olds are typically viewed as active individuals, Fisher's need for constant motion seems to be well above the normal range. This behavior has an impact on his ability to participate and learn in preschool. Fisher cannot sit for more than a minute. He spends circle time running around the tables in the back of the room. During center time, he moves quickly from center to center, without showing much interest in the materials. Fisher is demonstrating SPD in the area of vestibular (movement and balance) input. He is under-stimulated by movement and balance. Therefore, Fisher's brain needs more movement input than normal. Fisher cannot seem to get enough movement, thus seeking more by moving around constantly.

Sensory Processing Disorder and Related Terms

Some of the terminology related to sensory integration (SI) can be misused and confusing. For example, you may have heard a parent say, "My child has sensory integration."

Everyone has "sensory integration," while some children have difficulty with SI. Ayres labeled the group of sensory integration problems sensory integration dysfunction, which is sometimes called Sensory Integration Disorder. Many researchers in the field of sensory integration use SPD to describe this group of problems. To be current in the field, the authors use Sensory Processing Disorder (SPD) throughout this book.

Impact of Sensory Processing Disorder on Learning

The brain of a child with SPD works differently from that of a child who has no sensory integration issues. Because SPD affects the child's overall development, his participation in typical childhood experiences will be lacking, inconsistent, or ineffective. Performing ordinary life activities may be challenging for the child with SPD because the child's brain is unable to organize and process sensory information.

Sensory integration (SI) has an enormous impact on children's learning. Young children gain an understanding of the world through interaction with the environment. For example, a child digs a hole in the dirt. Through this process he learns many things, such as the texture and weight of the soil and which animals live in the soil, while he practices small motor skills. A child who has SPD is not able to organize sensory information and respond to input in a functional manner. These sensory processing difficulties cause the child to demonstrate negative behaviors or extreme emotions that are not the result of poor intellectual ability. As a result of SPD, a number of problems with learning, motor development, or behavior may be observed in preschool children, including the following:

❖ coordination problems;
❖ poor attention span or difficulty focusing on tasks;
❖ academic-related problems such as poor handwriting and difficulty cutting with scissors;
❖ problems with self-care skills such as tying shoes, zipping, buttoning, and feeding;
❖ low self-esteem;
❖ over-sensitivity to touch, sights, or sounds; and
❖ unusually high or low activity level.

A child who is overwhelmed by the sensory information from his environment will be unable to learn effectively. On the other hand, a child who is under-stimulated by the environment will also lack the input necessary to learn. The information in the next chapters will further describe sensory processing, which is necessary to provide the optimum learning environment for a variety of preschoolers. All young children can benefit from an environment designed with an awareness of the role that the senses play in their development.

Sensory Avoiders, Sensory Seekers, and Sensory Under-Responders

CHAPTER 2

Preschoolers with Sensory Processing Disorder

The child with Sensory Processing Disorder has a brain that experiences great difficulty with adjusting to or regulating responses to sensory inputs. This means that a child either does not react strongly enough or reacts too strongly to sensory input from the environment. The child who does not react strongly enough to sensory information is called under-responsive, while the child who reacts too strongly to sensory information is considered over-responsive.

Sensory Avoider

The Sensory Avoider is over-responsive to sensations from one or more sensory systems (touch, visual, auditory, movement and balance, body position, taste, and smell). Sensory Avoidance is the most common type of sensory problem. This child's brain is unable to effectively reduce sensations. The child may be over-aroused and may respond to certain sensory information as if it were irritating or painful; this child may even be afraid of many sensations (Miller & Fuller, 2006).

Some Sensory Avoiders are passive and try to get away from objects or activities that are frightening for them. They may choose to do a less frightening activity or "talk their way out of it." For example, the Sensory Avoider may stay away from the swings and the slide on the playground and choose to play in the sandbox every day.

Other Sensory Avoiders may be overly aggressive or forceful in their responses to sensations. They may react with inappropriate behaviors, such as hitting, biting, or kicking. Being removed from a situation due to a negative behavior helps the child avoid overwhelming sensory situations. The adult removing the child from the situation may be a way for the Sensory Avoider to get out of threatening situations. The child may prefer being removed to being urged to participate in an over-stimulating activity.

Tactile Avoidance or "tactile defensiveness" is a frequently identified type of sensory avoidance. This child reacts to tactile (touch) experiences in an extremely negative manner. For example, when introduced to a bowl containing a mixture of cornstarch and water ("goop"), four-year-old Damien's brain is telling him to avoid the new tactile experience. Damien hides under the table. When the teacher helps him back to his seat, Damien cries and screams, "I don't want to!" After much coaxing, Damien finally settles down. However, when asked to "try to touch the goop," Damien's response may be to pull away from the teacher's arm.

There are other types of Sensory Avoiders. Some children avoid sounds. They may hide or cover their ears and scream in response to certain sounds. Preschoolers who are Vestibular (movement) Avoiders are afraid to move, and so they may refuse to climb, swing, or ride on outdoor playground equipment. You may find these children sitting under a tree or canopy instead.

Sensory Seeker

The child who is a Sensory Seeker craves excessive stimulation from one or more of the sensory systems (touch, visual, auditory, movement and balance, body awareness, taste, and smell). This child seeks more stimulation than other children and never seems to be satisfied with the amount of sensory stimulation she receives (Miller & Fuller, 2006).

One type of Sensory Seeker may crave touch inputs. Elizabeth is a three-year-old child who brings a variety of stuffed animals to preschool each day. Although she has been told that her toys from home need to stay in her cubby, she retrieves them eight or nine times a day. She can be found rubbing the stuffed animals up

The Sensory
Under-Responder
gives less of a
response to
sensory input than
other children
and may react
very slowly or
need especially
strong inputs
before he or she
will respond.

and down her arms. Elizabeth still puts objects in her mouth and sucks her fingers. She is the first person to hop into the sandbox, and she removes her shoes and socks to touch the sand. Elizabeth's favorite center is art, where she insists on fingerpainting on her body rather than using the brushes or paper. The messier the activity, the more she likes it.

Other Sensory Seekers crave movement experiences. Teachers may describe a child in this category as a risk taker who is in constant motion. On the playground, she attempts to climb to the top of the swing set so she can jump off. She hangs upside down on the monkey bars and releases to fall on the ground. She wants you to push her swing higher and higher. You must constantly remind her of the rule about not jumping out of swings because she has done this numerous times. In the classroom, this child has a difficult time staying still, especially during quiet activities. At circle time, she stands up and sits down many times, or rocks or bounces herself. During center time, she seems to move around the classroom at top speed.

Some Sensory Seekers crave sound, taste, or smell inputs. A child who seeks auditory inputs may talk loudly, may hum to herself, or belch frequently. This child may also place a CD player to her ear and turn the volume as loud as possible. A child who seeks smell input may sniff her teachers and friends.

Sensory Under-Responders

The child with Under-Responsivity does not seem to notice inputs from one or more sensory system (touch, visual, auditory, movement and balance, body position, taste, and smell). This child gives less of a response to sensory input than other children and may react very slowly or need especially strong inputs before she will respond (Miller & Fuller, 2006).

Many Under-Responders do not react to other children touching or bumping into them. These children may not seem to notice when they get minor injuries such as cuts or bruises. For instance, a child whose parents report that she burned her hand on the outdoor grill but never cried, is a child who is most likely an Under-Responder.

Some preschoolers who are Under-Responders do not interact or play well with their peers. This child is often quiet and withdrawn. She may prefer solitary play activities such as looking at books or listening to music in the Library Center. When another child comes over to ask her to join in a play experience, she may respond with "I'm reading right now." Or she may ignore the other child completely.

The Under-Responder may be difficult for preschool teachers to identify because she is often quiet and passive. This is the child who may seem to be "in her own little world" and is unaware of other things that are going on in the classroom. She may be especially slow to respond to requests. As a result, she lacks the social skills needed to interact effectively with her peers.

Some children are under-responsive to vestibular or proprioceptive inputs. They do not seem to want to play or move around. Outside they may sit alone or wander around the playground. These children may appear very clumsy in comparison to other preschoolers. Some Under-Responders seem to be unaware of visual and auditory inputs in the environment including new visual images, objects, or sounds.

Some children seek out one type of sensation and avoid another type of sensory input.

Comparison of Sensory Avoiders, Sensory Seekers, and Sensory Under-Responders

Sensory Avoiders, the Sensory Seekers, and the Sensory Under-Responders react to sensory inputs in an atypical manner. The Sensory Avoider responds too much; the Sensory Seeker craves more and more; and the Sensory Under-Responder responds too little.

It is possible for one child to have Sensory Avoider characteristics and Sensory Seeker characteristics. Some children seek out one type of sensation and avoid another type of sensory input. For example, Lucas seeks out movement and balance (vestibular) experiences, but he also has tactile defensiveness and avoids light, unexpected touch and messy activities. Lucas is on one side of the spectrum for vestibular inputs and the other side of the spectrum for tactile sensations.

Identifying Sensory Avoiders, Sensory Seekers, and Sensory Under-Responders

The following sections are designed to help you recognize some typical subcategories of sensory processing disorder (SPD) in young children. This book includes sections related to seekers, avoiders, and under-responders in the following areas: visual, auditory, tactile, vestibular (movement and balance), and proprioceptive (body position) senses. Remember that the symptoms described will vary among children. No child will have all of these symptoms. However, if a child demonstrates several of the symptoms in one or more category, it is likely that she has some degree of SPD. For quick reference, all of the SPD red flags in this chapter are reprinted in the appendix on pages 136-140. These may be photocopied and posted in the classroom.

When you suspect a child has an SPD, remember:
- ❖ No child will have every symptom listed.
- ❖ Sensory processing can vary from day to day or moment to moment. It may be a good sensory processing day or a bad sensory processing day. Consider the context of the behavior.
- ❖ A child with SPD will probably have difficulty with more than one sensory input (tactile, vestibular, proprioceptive, visual, auditory, taste, or smell).
- ❖ It is possible that some children are sensory avoiding in one area and sensory seeking in another area.
- ❖ No two children are alike. Each child will demonstrate her own sensory integration (SI) skills and deficits.

Note: For additional guidelines, see Kranowitz, C. S. (2006). *The Out-of-Sync Child: Recognizing and Coping with Sensory Processing Disorder, Revised Edition.*

Visual Avoider: What Does This Child Do?

Augusta is a five-year-old girl in a kindergarten classroom. Augusta's mother reports that she knows the letters of the alphabet and can identify all the letter sounds. However, her teacher has yet to see Augusta copy a letter onto her paper. For example, when the teacher asks Augusta to "read the room" and try to find a word that begins with the letter "S," Augusta looks around the room and appears to be "distraught" over the entire process. Augusta eventually gives up. She sits down at her table, lays her head on her arms, and rubs her eyes with her hands. When the teacher asks Augusta for the sound that the letter "S" makes, Augusta answers correctly.

Augusta may be a Visual Avoider. Augusta's brain is not able to effectively integrate sensory information that comes through her eyes, and she is easily over-stimulated by visual input. Augusta's classroom is like many preschool classes—filled with artwork, centers, bright fluorescent lighting, and a lot of busy children. The teacher has worked diligently to label many items in the classroom. Augusta is not able to "read the room" to search for the letter "S," because the room is too visually stimulating for her. Her eyes hurt when she scans the environment to look for the "S." So, she closes her eyes to avoid getting too much visual input. Augusta can tell the teacher the sound the letter "S" makes, because that is an auditory skill and does not require her to look at anything.

Visual Avoider: Red Flags

Note: If you suspect a child may have SPD in the visual area, the child should have a thorough vision screening with an optometrist to rule out basic vision problems.

The Visual Avoider may

* avoid sunlight and other bright light (for example, the child may want to wear sunglasses or hat inside and outside);
* refuse to participate in activities where there are too many children involved (because the children are moving around and stimulating the visual system);
* get motion sickness from too much visual input;
* avoid eye contact with adults or peers;
* be unable to determine distances (for example, the child may bump into a bookcase or room divider);
* have headaches or nausea when she has overused her eyes;
* close her eyes or try to avoid balls or other objects thrown to her; or
* rub her eyes.

Visual Seeker: What Does This Child Do?

Maria's preschool teacher, Ms. Lisa, is concerned because Maria wants to sit at the computer during all free-choice and center times. Maria sits extremely close to the computer screen. Ms. Lisa encourages Maria to get involved in other centers, but Maria eventually moves back to the Library and Technology Center. Even when another child is using the computer, Maria will pull up a chair and stare blankly at the screen.

Maria may be a Visual Seeker who is using the computer screen to stimulate her sensory system. While most people may get tired of looking at a computer screen after a period of time, Maria is under-stimulated by visual information and seems to crave the visual stimulation the screen provides.

Visual Seeker: Red Flags

Note: If you suspect a child may have SPD in the visual area, the child should have a thorough vision screening with an optometrist to rule out basic vision problems.

The Visual Seeker may
- stare at bright lights, flickering lights, or direct sunlight;
- stare at her fingers as she moves them or at objects moving in space (for example, ceiling fans, flags, or mobiles);
- move around or shake her head during drawing or fine motor activities; or
- hold objects close to her face to look at them.

Visual Under-Responder: What Does This Child Do?

Marco is a four-year-old boy who attends a preschool program at an elementary school. Over the weekend Mrs. Suite set up a new learning center: "The Bakery." At morning circle, Mrs. Suite begins her introduction of "The Bakery." She asks the children, "Does anyone see anything new in our room today?" All the children, except Marco, excitedly raise their hands. Marco, who is doing his "usual zoning out," does not respond. So, Mrs. Suite asks, "Marco, what can you tell me about our new center?" Marco responds, "What new center?" The other children begin bouncing up and down and saying, "I can." "I can." Mrs. Suite points towards "The Bakery" and says, "Over there, Marco." Marco says, "Oh, I don't know. I didn't see it."

Marco may be a Visual Under-Responder. Marco's brain is not able to effectively integrate visual sensory information, and he is under-responsive to that input. Marco did not notice the change in the classroom environment because his sensory system responds too slowly to visual input. He is not visually alert and aware of new visual information and seems to lack interest in the world around him.

Visual Under-Responder: Red Flags

Note: If you suspect a child may have SPD in the visual area, the child should have a thorough vision screening with an optometrist to rule out basic vision problems.

The Visual Under-Responder may
- ❖ be unaware of new objects, materials or people in the environment;
- ❖ stare at bright lights or moving objects with a faraway look in her eyes;
- ❖ fall over or bump into new obstacles inside or outside; or
- ❖ have difficulty catching balls or getting out of the way of moving objects or people because she responds too slowly.

Auditory Avoider: What Does This Child Do?

Ethan is a three-year-old child whose mother has just returned to work; he now attends a full-day child care center. Ethan's teacher has observed that he gets very upset each time the train passes by the center and blows its whistle, which happens four times a day. Most of the children either race to the window to watch the train or completely ignore it. Ethan runs to a corner, cowers down, covers his ears, and closes his eyes as though afraid. Ethan's teacher reported this behavior to his mother, who said, "Yes, he is very sensitive to loud noises. He hides in his closet every time I vacuum at home. So, I just don't vacuum when he is there."

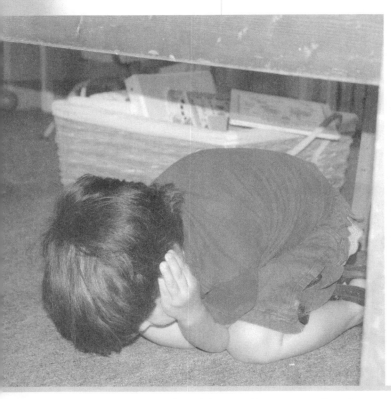

Ethan may be an Auditory Avoider. He is over-sensitive to loud noises like the whistle on the train and the vacuum cleaner. These sounds may actually be painful to Ethan. Some children who have auditory defensiveness say that hearing certain sounds feels like getting an injection in their ear. Ethan's brain cannot effectively integrate the auditory input, so Ethan attempts to avoid the sound of the train by hiding and covering his ears.

Auditory Avoider: Red Flags

The Auditory Avoider may

❖ demonstrate excessive emotions (for example, crying, screaming, anger) when she hears a sudden noise such as an alarm, thunder, siren, or horn;

❖ demonstrate excessive emotions when the noise level in the room increases (for example, during center time);

❖ put her fingers in her ears and yell or hum, to drown out certain sounds (for example, a train);

❖ be upset by common noises such as a that of a toilet flushing, water running, or background music; or

❖ demonstrate excessive emotions when she hears high-pitched sounds such as a drill, whistle, chalk squeaking, or metal clinking.

Auditory Seeker: What Does This Child Do?

Kaitlynn is a four-year-old girl in a Title 1 preschool program at her local elementary school. She has a diagnosis of Developmental Delay, but Kaitlynn's teacher suspects that she may be autistic. Kaitlynn does not actively participate at circle time; she does not make eye contact with her teacher; she typically sits in the circle, rocking back and forth and humming loudly to herself; and she often escapes to the bathroom, where she closes the door and flushes the toilet repeatedly. Her favorite center is the Music Center, where she puts on headphones and listens to music with the CD player set on its loudest volume.

Kaitlynn may be an Auditory Seeker. Kaitlynn actively seeks auditory input by wearing headphones and turning the volume as loud as possible. Her brain craves more and more auditory input. Common sounds, such as the

Kobe does not follow his teacher's verbal requests because his sensory system does not organize that auditory input and respond appropriately.

toilet flushing, are interesting to Kaitlynn, as she derives pleasure from listening to them. The sound of her teacher talking or singing during circle time is not stimulating enough for Kaitlynn's auditory system, so she hums to herself at the same time.

Auditory Seeker: Red Flags

Note: If you suspect a child may be an Auditory Seeker, the child should have a thorough auditory screening to rule out basic hearing problems.

The Auditory Seeker may

❖ turn the volume of music up very loud;

❖ talk very loudly inside the classroom;

❖ hold musical toys or other toys that make noise directly to her ear to listen;

❖ make noisy sounds such as clapping, yelling, banging objects, or singing loudly;

❖ enjoy high-pitched noises (such as a drill, a whistle, or bells); or

❖ crave common noises such as that of a toilet flushing, water running, or an air conditioner humming.

Auditory Under-Responder: What Does This Child Do?

Kobe recently moved into the four-year-old classroom. During the transition meeting, Kobe's former teacher, Mrs. Lee, reported that Kobe's biggest problem is his inability to follow directions. She stated, "He just ignores me. I can't get him to do anything. I can call him by name four or five times, but it's like he doesn't even hear me. When it is time to go to the bathroom or go outside, I have to take his hand and guide him. Then he just follows right along with me."

Kobe may be an Auditory Under-Responder. He does not follow his teacher's verbal requests because his sensory system does not organize that auditory input and respond appropriately. Kobe may not hear Mrs. Lee's voice in the midst of all the other noises in the classroom. When Mrs. Lee physically prompts Kobe by holding his hand, he follows along.

Kobe is not "ignoring" Mrs. Lee, but his auditory system is not processing that information correctly.

Auditory Under-Responder: Red Flags

Note: If you suspect a child may be an Auditory Under-Responder, the child should have a thorough auditory screening to rule out basic hearing problems.

The Auditory Under-Responder may
* seem unaware of typical sounds in the classroom or outside;
* respond slowly or not at all to verbal requests; or
* pay attention only to extremely loud noises or music that is boisterous or has an unusual rhythm.

Tactile Avoider: What Does This Child Do?

Adrianna has just started attending preschool in a child care facility. A bright child with good language skills, Adrianna appears to be unhappy in her new class. She rarely smiles and has not established any relationships with her peers.

Adrianna is a very picky eater with a limited diet consisting of soft foods, such as mashed potatoes, bread, bananas, yogurt, and pudding. Her mother packs lunch for Adrianna, but she usually just sits and stares while the other children eat. At rest time, Adrianna tosses and turns on her mat, readjusts her blanket over and over again, and usually falls asleep during the last 15–20 minutes of rest time. She awakens irritable and wanders aimlessly around the classroom while the other children eat a snack.

Adrianna never chooses the Art Center and refuses to participate in messy activities. When the class planted tomato plants in their outside pots, Adrianna clung to the teacher and said, "Yuck! I don't want to do it!" When another child accidentally bumped into Adrianna, while carrying a pitcher of water, and spilled some on her leg, Adrianna cried and screamed at the top of her lungs, "Aah! He spilled water on me!"

After 10 minutes of crying, an assistant teacher was forced to separate Adrianna from the rest of the children.

Adrianna may be a Tactile Avoider ("tactile defensive"). Her sensory system is unable to process certain touch inputs, like textured foods. Even simple, everyday activities, such as eating, can be overwhelming for Adrianna. Her brain is especially over-stimulated by messy experiences, such as planting in the dirt, where Adrianna is afraid and attempts to avoid the activity. When another child bumps into her and spills water on her leg, Adrianna's sensory system is overloaded, her brain says, "Ouch! That hurt!" and she responds by crying.

Tactile Avoider: Red Flags

The Tactile Avoider may

❖ respond to light or unexpected touch in a negative manner (for example, hitting, biting) or with excessive emotions (for example, crying, screaming);

❖ avoid messy activities in the classroom (for example, painting, gluing);

❖ run away or hide when a tactile experience is introduced;

❖ not like to be kissed or touched, but may initiate hugs or firm touch;

❖ walk at the front or end of the line to avoid being touched;

❖ be a picky eater;

❖ be very clean and wash her hands immediately after any activity;

❖ appear stubborn or inflexible;

❖ be excessively ticklish;

❖ dislike going barefoot;

❖ react with extreme emotion or anger when face is washed;

❖ refuse to hold hands with someone else;

❖ overreact to minor bumps, cuts, or scrapes;

❖ complain about certain types of clothing or tags in shirts;

- ❖ require that her shoes be tied extra tight, or complain about socks being bunched or twisted;
- ❖ try to talk her way out of touching or playing with textures: "My mommy told me not to get my new dress dirty;"
- ❖ have difficulty establishing friendships in the classroom, because she stays away from other children to avoid getting touched unexpectedly or lightly;
- ❖ walk on tiptoes; or
- ❖ refuse to wear hats or dress-up clothes.

Tactile (Touch) Seeker: What Does This Child Do?

Jacob is a four-year-old child who attends a pre-K program in an elementary school. No matter how often his teacher says, "Keep your hands to yourself," Jacob just cannot stop touching his friends. While standing in line, Jacob constantly bumps into other children, rubs, pokes, or pushes them. During circle time, Jacob sits in a child-size chair to keep him from rolling all over the mat and other children. While sitting, Jacob twists his hair with one or both hands. By the end of the day, Jacob is always dirty. His favorite outside activity is the sandbox. Even if it is wet, he plays in the sand. Jacob will sit in the sandbox and pour sand over his arms and legs. In the Art Center, Jacob paints his body rather than the paper. He dips his fingers into glue and, after it has dried, slowly peels it off. Jacob's shirt is usually wet, because he chews on the collar, hem, or sleeve throughout the day.

Jacob may be a Tactile Seeker who craves tactile input because he is under-stimulated by touch, which means that it takes an excessive amount of tactile input before Jacob's brain can register that he has been touched. Therefore, he constantly touches himself, things, and other people. He rolls around on the floor during circle time because his body needs excessive tactile input to stay alert and help him pay attention. Like all preschoolers, Jacob learns about his environment by touching and manipulating objects, while taking the experiences a step further, to be able to really learn. So, instead of just playing in the sandbox, Jacob pours the sand over his skin.

Tactile Seeker: Red Flags

The Tactile Seeker may
- appear to crave touch (for example, the child will fingerpaint for a long time);
- constantly put objects in her mouth;
- love messy experiences;
- bump into things or people;
- be unable to keep her hands to herself;
- stuff her mouth with food;
- rub textures over her arms or legs;
- prefer spicy, hot, or very cold foods;
- get very close to others when playing or talking;
- rub or bite her own skin; or
- touch others constantly.

Tactile Under-Responder: What Does This Child Do?

Mariah is a three-year-old child who attends a church preschool program three days a week. Mariah is a "loner" who does not play with the other three-year-olds. Although she is almost four, she still wears diapers to preschool and does not tell the teacher when she needs to go potty. During center time, Mariah typically chooses the Library Center, where she sits quietly and looks at books.

When the class is doing creative art experiences, Mariah appears disinterested. After much prompting, Mariah will join in the activity. However, she has a very difficult time manipulating the paintbrush, markers, or scissors. She tends to get the materials all over her, but never fusses or requests to wash her hands.

Mariah demonstrates characteristics that are common for children who are Tactile Under-Responders. Mariah's sensory system does not respond to typical touch inputs such as paint on her hands. Mariah is not potty trained because her brain is slow to register the need to go to the bathroom or the feeling of a wet diaper. She has difficulty with small motor activities because she doesn't feel the tools or materials in her hand the same way that other children do. Mariah's brain needs stronger or longer-lasting touch input before it will be aware of that tactile information.

Mariah is not potty trained because her brain is slow to register the need to go to the bathroom or the feeling of a wet diaper.

Tactile Under-Responder: Red Flags

The Tactile Under-Responder may

❖ seem unaware of a messy or dirty face or body;

❖ not respond to gentle touches;

❖ lack interest in creative arts (for example, paint, glue, clay);

❖ have difficulty manipulating small toys or objects;

❖ not seem to notice cold or hot temperature;

❖ seem unaware of different textures (for example, hard, scratchy, soft);

❖ not notice that clothing is wet or dirty;

❖ be slow with potty-training; or

❖ be slow to learn how to undress/dress self.

Vestibular (Movement and Balance) Avoider: What Does This Child Do?

Evan is a talkative five-year-old boy. Each morning, Evan enters his preschool classroom carrying a bag of cereal and a soft drink. His mother reports that this "keeps Evan from throwing up" during their 20-minute commute. Once Evan finishes his morning snack, he typically goes to the Library Center, where he will read to himself and sometimes drift off to sleep.

Evan plays more with the girls than the boys in his class. On the playground, Rachel and Mimi play "family" with him. Evan follows them around from place to place. When the girls climb up the ladder to the tree house, Evan stays at the bottom, saying, "I'm going to mow the yard." Eventually, Evan sits down under a tree and pushes mulch around until it is time to go in for lunch.

Evan is the first to wash his hands and sit at the lunch table. Several boys sit near him. Will talks about his birthday party, which is planned for an indoor playground, and says to Evan, "I invited you, too. It's gonna be so cool!" Evan responds with, "I don't like that place. I probably can't go." Will reacts by saying, "Well, I didn't want you to come anyway!"

Evan may be a Vestibular Avoider because his brain is easily over-stimulated by movement. Evan cannot ride in the car to school without becoming carsick, because the movement overloads his sensory system.

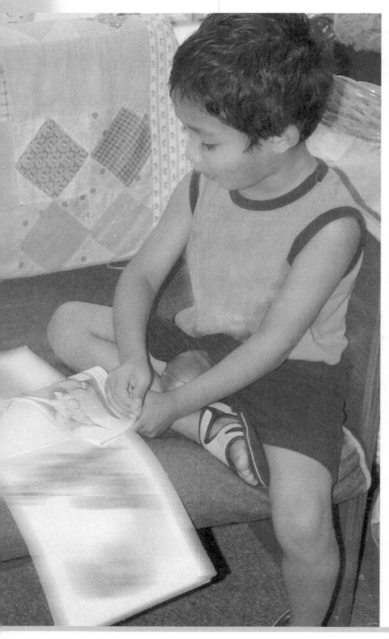

When he arrives at school, Evan's sensory system wants to shut down, and it tells his body that it is time to sleep. Drowsiness or sleep is a common reaction to vestibular over-stimulation. On the playground, Evan avoids playground equipment, such as slides and swings, and talks his way out of climbing the ladder by inventing pretend play activities limited to the ground (mowing the grass). Evan does not participate in many large motor activities and is clumsy and uncoordinated, which influences his social interactions with his peers and lowers his self-esteem.

Vestibular Avoider: Red Flags

The Vestibular Avoider may
* be timid and cautious with movement experiences (a non-risk taker);
* be fearful of playground equipment such as slides, swings, jungle gyms, or monkey bars;
* get carsick, even on short trips;
* have poor self-esteem, because she will not play with others, particularly outside;
* be afraid of elevators or escalators;

- be fearful of heights or dislike when her feet are off the ground;
- be afraid to climb or descend stairs (for example, hold the railing with both hands);
- appear stubborn or uncooperative;
- be unable to ride a tricycle, bicycle, or other age-appropriate riding toys;
- appear manipulative, especially in cases where she feels a lack of control (For example, the child may say, "Let's go play under the tree. Only babies go on the slide."); or
- be clumsy or uncoordinated.

Vestibular (Movement and Balance) Seeker: What Does This Child Do?

"Pablo goes nonstop!" says Ms. Beverly, his teacher. He is constantly moving—from the time he walks in the door, he is always on the go. Pablo has a lot of trouble sitting down during morning circle time. Ms. Beverly has tried everything she can think of to encourage him to sit still, but nothing works. Even when he is sitting in the circle, Pablo is still moving. He rocks back and forth and constantly fidgets with his pockets, buttons, or the ties on his clothes.

Pablo is a risk taker and gets hurt all the time. When asked about his participation in outside play, Ms. Beverly says, "The things he tries… oh, he just scares me. Once, when he was at home, he jumped off the top of his sister's playhouse and fell into some trees. He broke his arm in two places. I don't take my eyes off of him when we are outside."

Ms. Beverly is concerned about how to help Pablo pay attention and be more focused in the classroom. She states, "I have tried to use positive discipline and say things like, 'Pablo, your feet need to be on the ground,' when he walks across the chairs. But, it just does not seem to sink in."

Pablo may be a Vestibular Seeker. In order for Pablo's brain to comprehend that he is moving, he needs to take in a lot of intense vestibular input. Pablo's brain tells his body that he needs more movement. Pablo constantly participates in excessive amounts or

> **In order for Pablo's brain to comprehend that he is moving, he needs to take in a lot of intense vestibular input.**

extreme types of movement experiences. Pablo appears to be a risk taker or troublemaker, judging from his actions, such as jumping off the top of a playhouse for the movement experience of flying through the air. However, it is not Pablo's intention to make trouble.

Some children who are Vestibular Seekers may also have Attention Deficit Hyperactivity Disorder (ADHD), but not all of them do. Children who are Vestibular Seekers move constantly, because their brains need more input. Asking Pablo to sit still for the entire circle time is futile; he must keep moving so he can stay alert and attentive.

Vestibular Seeker: Red Flags

The Vestibular Seeker may

* take safety risks inside and outside;
* not be able to sit still;
* be impulsive (do things before thinking);
* run instead of walk;
* be in constant motion (for example, wiggle, fidget, rock back and forth, bounce on her bottom);
* push every movement experience to the extreme (for example, attempt to swing over the top of the swing set);
* not get dizzy, no matter how much she has been spinning around; or
* enjoy movement experiences more than other children.

Vestibular (Movement and Balance) Under-Responder: What Does This Child Do?

Ms. Ann Marie is worried about Gatlin. Gatlin is very quiet and withdrawn. It almost seems like he just doesn't have the energy to participate in the classroom. He takes a good nap and eats well. But, he is slow to move around the classroom and sometimes just looks as though he is daydreaming. Ms. Ann Marie thought maybe Gatlin wasn't getting enough rest at home so she asked Gatlin's mother about his daily routine. She reported that Gatlin is a "very good sleeper" and has always been the "best child."

Gatlin typically ignores his peers and rarely joins them in play, even if they have requested that he do so. When they are on the playground, Gatlin usually sits under the play structure, digging in the mulch. But, if Ms. Ann Marie goes with him to the swings, he will swing as long as she will push him. Gatlin is the last one to get into line when the class transitions back inside, moving slowly and shuffling his feet in an uncoordinated fashion.

Gatlin may be a Vestibular Under-Responder. Gatlin responds less to classroom or playground experiences than is typical for other children his age. For instance, instead of running and playing outside on the playground, Gatlin prefers to sit and watch. In the classroom, Gatlin spends time "daydreaming" rather than exploring the classroom or interacting with his peers.

Although Gatlin does not move a lot, he is different than a Vestibular Avoider. He is not afraid to move. It just takes Gatlin longer to react to movement experiences, and his brain may require more intense movement input before he will respond. For instance, once Ms. Ann Marie gets him started swinging, he enjoys the movement experience.

Vestibular Under-Responder: Red Flags

The Vestibular Under-Responder may

* appear accident prone (for example, falls or trips and does not catch himself);
* be less coordinated than other preschoolers;
* not notice movements or changes in movement (for example, pushing high on a swing);
* not like new movement experiences;
* tend to sit, stand, or lay around more than other preschoolers; or
* appear easily tired or lazy.

Proprioception Avoider: What Does This Child Do?

Ann is a well-behaved child who never causes any trouble in her preschool. In fact, she seems to disappear inside the classroom. Her favorite spot is the "comfy chair" in the Quiet Place Center. She stays there, never moving, for the full 45 minutes of center time each morning. When it is time to transition to lunch, a teacher usually has to help Ann out of the chair.

Ann is always the last one to lunch, walking slowly at the end of the line. She is overweight and has poor posture. Ann also has unusual food preferences; she will eat fruits, pudding, and other soft foods, but does not like crunchy foods, like raw vegetables, or chewy foods, such as peanut butter-and-jelly sandwiches. After lunch, Ann is always ready for a rest. While she does not like her teacher to help put the sheet on her mat, Ann typically struggles with the task for a moment, gives up, and just lays the sheet on top of the mat.

Ann may be a Proprioception Avoider. She does not like to participate in activities that are hard to do. The sense of proprioception (body position) is achieved through stretch input to joints and muscles of the body. Ann receives too much proprioceptive input while doing heavy work activities, such as climbing a tree or pushing a box full of blocks across the carpet. Ann does not want her teacher to help her with the mat cover because she does not like the deep pressure of her teacher's hands on her arms, and she does not eat crunchy or chewy foods because they require hard work to eat.

Children who avoid proprioceptive (deep pressure) input often appear lazy. Ann usually chooses to relax in a comfortable chair rather than build with blocks or play in the Home Living Center; moving heavy blocks or pushing a baby doll stroller is hard work. Ann is a slow mover because the faster she walks or runs the more input she gives her joints and muscles. Ann's brain tells her body to avoid heavy work because it is too hard.

Proprioception Avoider: Red Flags

The Proprioception Avoider may

* appear lazy or overly tired;
* avoid physical activities (running, jumping, skipping, or hopping);
* be a picky eater;
* prefer not to move; or
* dislike other people moving her body (not want you to help her place her arms into her coat).

Proprioception (Body Position) Seeker: What Does This Child Do?

Parker is an energetic four-year-old boy who entertains himself by running and crashing into walls, bookcases, and the water fountain. After he falls down, Parker jumps up from the floor and laughs wildly at himself. He never seems to get hurt. The girls in his classroom run away when they see Parker coming. Parker chases the girls until his teacher calls to him.

Most of the children are afraid of Parker because he is so rough. He sometimes pushes and hits them, especially at the end of the day when everyone is tired. Parker has only one close friend, Raphael. The two boys like to "rough house" on the playground, even as the teacher reminds them of the "no wrestling" rule at school.

Parker may be a Proprioception Seeker. He needs proprioceptive (body position) input from heavy work activities or movements that provide a stretch of his muscles. It takes Parker's brain more input than usual to understand what his body parts are doing. Parker's brain tells his body to "Give me more!" As a result, Parker crashes into things, wrestles with

Raphael, and pushes heavy objects around because it gives him the deep pressure input his brain craves.

Parker appears aggressive with other children because he hurtles into them with such great force. Parker does not do these things to gain attention. Rather, he hits and pushes to get more deep pressure input. His participation in rough play has a negative impact on relationships with his peers, as most other children do not want to play roughly with him. Parker needs help to find more appropriate ways for getting deep pressure input and be more aware of his body.

Proprioception Seeker: Red Flags

The Proprioception Seeker may
- ❖ enjoy crashing into walls, objects, or people;
- ❖ bite her fingernails or suck her thumb or fingers;
- ❖ demonstrate aggressive behaviors such as hitting, kicking, or biting;
- ❖ be unaware of other person's personal space (get in your face when she is talking or lie on you when you are sitting);
- ❖ request that you tie her shoes very tightly;
- ❖ stomp her feet when walking;
- ❖ chew on objects, including her shirt, pencils, markers, toys, and gum;
- ❖ like to be patted very firmly or wrapped tightly in a blanket during rest time; or
- ❖ participate in rough-and-tumble play that is extremely forceful.

Proprioception (Body Position) Under-Responder: What Does This Child Do?

Phillipe attends a Head Start Program. Phillipe is a very pleasant four-year-old child who will soon be five. Phillipe's least favorite activity is morning circle, where the teacher often guides the children in movement activities with music. Phillipe will sit in his chair until a classroom aide lifts him to his feet. Then he just stands in place as the other children move around him.

Phillipe is clumsy. He did not learn to walk until he was almost two years old. Now, he walks with an unusual gait: locking his knees into place as he goes. He often falls at school, but he has never cried. Last week he fell down the stairs of his home and his grandmother reported that, "He didn't even cry."

Phillipe has delays in fine motor skills and self-care skills. He holds a pencil in the palm of his hand and cannot copy a square or triangle. He can snip with scissors, but is not able to cut a straight line. Phillipe has only been potty trained for two months and still wears a pull-up during rest time. He has great difficulty using a spoon and fork and gets the food all over him. His grandmother still feeds him at home.

Phillipe demonstrates characteristics that are common for children who are Proprioception Under-Responders. Phillipe does not have the inner desire to want to move his body. His brain is slow to interpret the signals coming from his muscles and joints. Phillipe's brain does not register the position of his head, hands, arms, legs, and feet like a typical brain does. So, learning new motor skills is more challenging for him. When Phillipe does move, it is often uncoordinated. As a result, Phillipe is delayed in some of his motor skills. He also does not want to participate in new movement experiences such as dancing to the music during morning circle.

Proprioception Under-Responder: Red Flags

The Proprioception Under-Responder may:
- ❖ not be aware when someone bumps into her;
- ❖ have poor small motor skills (for example, cutting, drawing, writing, feeding);
- ❖ be slow to learn how to undress/dress self;
- ❖ be uncoordinated with large motor skills (for example, walking, running, hopping, skipping);
- ❖ not cry when significant injury occurs;

- ❖ appear disinterested in movement experiences; or
- ❖ break toys easily because she has difficulty manipulating objects.

Summary

Now that you know about some of the Sensory Processing Disorders (SPD) that may have an impact on young children, you must learn what to do next. The following sections offer suggestions on observing children in the preschool setting to identify SPD and provide practical tips for discussing your suspicions about sensory processing problems with parents. Information regarding medical professionals who can make formal diagnoses is also included. Suggestions for ways to change the environment to meet the needs of children with SPD are included in the next chapters.

Observing Children

Many early childhood educators are keen observers of young children's behaviors. As a teacher of young children, you are in a position to detect sensory processing problems in children at a critical point in their development. Good sensory integration (SI) skills are required for a child to learn and function effectively. Therefore, it is critical that SPD be identified as early as possible so that appropriate intervention can begin.

Use the following suggestions to guide your observation of young children (Bundy, Lane & Murray, 2002). Remember to note the child's strengths as well as any weaknesses. A skillful teacher builds on a child's strengths to help improve the child's weak areas.

Begin the observation by considering a few general questions:
- ❖ How does the child respond to touch (for example, will she not participate in messy experiences or does she not like to get dirty)?
- ❖ How does the child react to movement experiences (for example, is she a risk taker on the playground or does she not play on outdoor equipment)?
- ❖ How does the child do with self-care activities, such as eating and dressing (for example, is she a very picky eater or a sloppy eater who gets overly messy)?

❖ How does the child move her body (for example, is she coordinated or clumsy, or is she always moving or moving very slowly)?

❖ How does the child get along with other children (for example, has she built strong friendships, or is she a loner)?

❖ How is the child's self-esteem (for example, does she make negative comments about herself, or is she confident in her skills)?

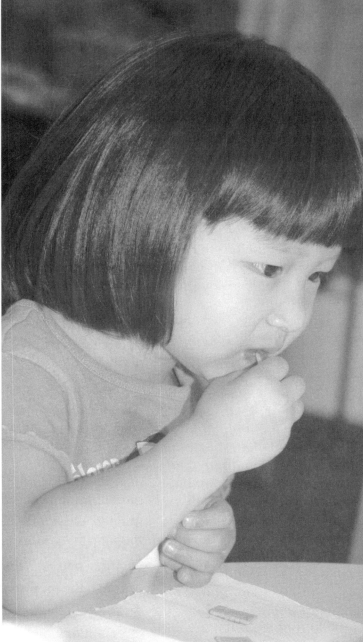

When you have a general idea about when or in what areas the child is having problems, refer to the red flags listed for each SPD discussed earlier in this chapter. You may also wish to use a screening tool to further expand your observations of the child. *Preschool SENSE: Sensory Scan for Educators* was designed by Carol S. Kranowitz (2006), author of *The Out-of-Sync Child: Recognizing and Coping with Sensory Processing Disorder, Revised Edition. Preschool SENSE* includes checklists to assist early childhood educators in recording their observations of preschool children who may have sensory processing disorder or problems.

It is helpful for you and for the child's parents to document the child's unusual behaviors or emotional responses. It may be particularly beneficial for medical professionals to have specific, written instances when a problem occurred. If possible, include what was going on immediately before or during the behavior; also include the date and time of the incident. The documentation can be brief—for example, "7/6/06, 10:00 AM: Fingerpainting with foam soap. Josh gagged when paint was squirted on the table. He did not touch."

Consider what goals you want the child to achieve in your classroom and document the goals. You may make a few long-term goals that can be accomplished by the end of the year. For example, "Josh will participate in 90% of art activities by the end of the year." You could also

Young children who receive quality early intervention have a greater probability of succeeding in school and in life.

make short-term goals that serve as stepping stones in helping the child achieve the larger goals, such as "Josh will paint with foam soap." Setting specific goals for the child will assist in assessment of any improvement that is made. The goals also help in your evaluation of changes or modifications that are made in the classroom. In addition, if the child qualifies for therapy, the occupational therapist (OT) will need to know your goals for the child, because these goals form the basis of an intervention plan for the child.

When to Refer and to Whom

The earlier a child is diagnosed as having SPD, the earlier intervention can begin. A young child's brain develops rapidly and has much flexibility during the first seven years of life, which means that intervention that begins during the preschool years has a better chance of improving a child's sensory processing skills. Young children who receive quality early intervention have a greater probability of succeeding in school and in life. Early diagnosis is a must, and you can play a very important part in the identification process.

If your observation reveals characteristics suggesting sensory processing problems, the child should receive a thorough evaluation by someone trained in the identification of SPD, such as a pediatric OT. The Individuals with Disabilities Education Act (IDEA) mandates that all children between the ages of three and five may receive assessments through the local school district or other designated program. Contact your local school district and ask for their preschool special education program or Child Find Program to learn about eligibility requirements and where the child can go to receive an assessment.

If the parents or guardians do not wish to have their child screened through the local school system, suggest one of the following medical professionals:

❖ Pediatric OT
❖ Pediatrician or other physician (M.D.) such as a developmental pediatrician or family practice physician
❖ Child clinical psychologist (Ph.D.)
❖ Child psychiatrist (M.D.)

Talking with Parents/Guardians

One of the most important roles of an early childhood educator is communicating effectively with a child's family. However, discussing a child's problems with her parents or guardians can be a very difficult task. Begin by scheduling a time to meet with the family when distractions are at a minimum. Be honest and sincere in your discussion. You may want to use the sandwich approach to discussing the child's performance in the class, meaning that you start with a few of the child's strengths, present the child's weaknesses, describe a few of the behaviors that concern you, and close with at least one more of the child's strengths. Keep your description of the negative aspects brief and to the point. It may help to have a short list of behaviors handy so you can refer to it. In this way, you reassure parents and guardians by emphasizing that the child has strengths, while letting them know of your concerns.

Inform the parents of your concern that their child *may* have SPD. Remind the parents that you do not diagnose problems, but that you are concerned about their child and how she is functioning in preschool.

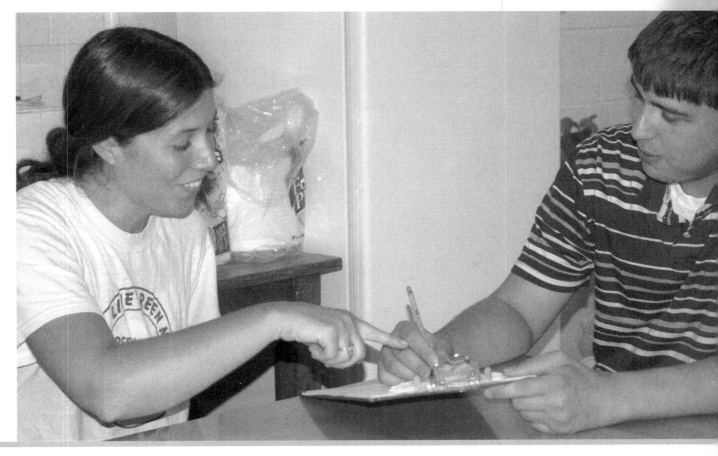

Once you have informed the parents, ask if they have questions for you. Then, listen to their responses. Be sympathetic. Your observations may be a big shock for the parents. If asked a question for which you have no answer, it is best to say that you don't know the answer. Recommend that the child receive a thorough evaluation by a health care professional trained in SI, such as a pediatric OT. Suggest that the parents ask that health care professional any questions you are unable to answer. It is very important to assure the parents that if their child has SPD, there are interventions that can help their child. Explain that the professional who completes the evaluation will recommend any intervention that is needed. Let the parents know that you support them and their child and that you want to be part of the process in whatever manner they find most appropriate.

Preschool teachers can help young children reach their fullest potential. Following the principles of SI theory, educators can make simple changes in the environment that will have a positive impact on young children's learning. The remaining chapters describe ways to provide a more organized and effective learning environment for all children.

Design the Environment to Support the Sensory Development of All Children

CHAPTER 3

Positive Effects of the Environment

As an early childhood teacher, you have the opportunity to have an enormous impact on young children because you work with them during a critical period in their development. The essential skills that you help a child develop during his first years will follow him throughout the rest of his life. A learning environment designed with careful consideration of children's sensory integration will be a more successful place for children to learn.

Following a logical plan of classroom design yields a greater potential for providing the "just-right challenge" for each child.

An effective environmental design incorporates the appropriate amount and type of sensory inputs for indoors and outdoors, taking various senses into consideration: lighting choices (visual), sound levels (auditory), arts and creative materials (tactile), and playground activities (vestibular and proprioceptive). Think about whether the environment will be over-stimulating or under-stimulating for each young child. Following a logical plan of classroom design yields a greater potential for providing the "just-right challenge" for each child.

The environment is ever-changing; it is important to assess the space and its impact on the child regularly. It is crucial to consider the environmental influences acting on a child who demonstrates challenging behaviors and reflect on how the environment impacts individual children and groups of young children when things work well. The positive effect of an environment on young children can be seen in many ways.

Use these questions to guide your observation of the environment:
❖ Is the child interacting and cooperating during play?
❖ Does the child appear attentive and interested in the materials?
❖ Does the child transition smoothly?
❖ Is the child engaged and alert when appropriate for the activity?
❖ Is the child calm and focused when appropriate for the activity?
❖ Does the child engage peers in learning activities and play?

When observing that the children are participating effectively in the physical environment, also note what is happening in the learning environment.

Role of the Teacher

The learning environment includes you, the teacher. You are the biggest influence on the child's educational environment. Your interactions with each child should be based on an understanding of the impact that sensory processing can have on their behavior. It is helpful to consider the effect your role as a teacher can have on creating a wonderful environment for children. There are several simple methods you can use to promote positive, sensory-smart interactions with the children in your classroom.

Monitor Your Voice Level

Speak with a low, calm voice. When children are very active and talkative, such as during center time, it is sometimes hard to gain their attention. In response, teachers may use a loud voice to get the children to hear. However, many children are over-stimulated by a loud, boisterous voice. Rather than paying attention to your words, these children will become even more excited or active in response to the volume of your voice. Remaining calm and using a quiet voice will entice most children to listen more carefully to what you are saying.

Follow a Routine

Young children need to follow a predictable schedule. Think about the last time there was a rainy day and the children could not go outside. Remember how hard it was for the children to participate in the indoor activity? Young children thrive in a consistent environment where they are informed of upcoming activities. Many preschoolers have difficulty remaining organized and attentive when their routine changes. For example, a preschooler might say, "We can't eat lunch. We haven't been outside."

Having a picture schedule (see Chapter 6 for instructions) of the daily routine is especially beneficial for young children. There will be days, however, that changes must be made. As soon as you become aware of a change occurring in the schedule, prepare the children by telling them about the "switcheroo." Talking about the change helps relieve anxiety or fear when the change happens.

Simplify Instructions

Children who have Sensory Processing Disorder (SPD) often need extra time to process new information. Make direct eye contact with the child to help him focus on your words. Use brief instructions and ask specific questions. Then allow the child time to think before responding. Repeat the question, if necessary. You can ask the child to restate the instructions to assure that he has heard you correctly.

Offer Appropriate Choices

Provide children with choices during the day. Open-ended materials such as clay, blocks, or paper allow a child to determine for himself how to use the objects. With some young preschoolers, a choice between two activities will be plenty. For example, "Would you like to paint or use clay?" More confident or experienced preschoolers may be able to decide between three or four choices, as is the case in classrooms that use a center-based design. A choice board, which clearly indicates the centers that are open and the number of children who can enter each center, is a helpful tool. The choice board provides children with the opportunity to make a selection that is appropriate to meet their sensory needs at that moment. For example, if Marley is feeling particularly "avoidant" of tactile input, he may choose the Manipulatives Center that has only two slots available. This may work better for him than the Block Center, which is open to four children.

For a child who is unable to make a decision between the numerous centers, you may limit his options by selecting two centers and pointing to the pictures of each. Then, ask the child to choose between the two. For example, "The Block Center and the Garden Center are open. Which center do you choose?"

Prevent Problems

Some "breakdowns" can be prevented through environmental design and careful observation of a child's behaviors. Each child will have some signs that indicate he is coming close to reaching his sensory limit. For example, a child may get sweaty or tearful before he falls apart completely. It is easier to prevent over-stimulation than to help the child get reorganized after he has been over-stimulated. For instance, if a preschooler is cowering under the table with his hands over his ears, it will be difficult for him to return to the activity. The child may have paced around the room prior to going under the table. If you observed this sign, you could have suggested that he put on headphones to keep the noise from hurting his ears. This change could have prevented the child from auditory over-stimulation.

When the child's individual signs are evident, stop and change something in the environment. Modification could include a simple step, such as removal of the child from the activity or giving the child a firm hug. Other changes might be more significant, such as giving the child a heavy work activity such as cleaning off the table tops with a clean, wet towel. This heavy work activity can help calm the child.

Instead of punishing the child for negative behavior, consider if there is something that needs to change in the environment. For a child who reacts to certain sensory input with aggressive behaviors, the response must include something to help the child become more focused and calm. Put on your "investigator's hat" to determine why the child is demonstrating the challenging behavior, and then respond. For example, a child who demonstrates sensory avoidance of vestibular input may attempt to avoid a movement experience, such as swinging, with verbal aggression toward another child. "You are a poo-poo head! I'm not swinging with you!" A response of taking the child off the playground further encourages the avoidant behavior, because being removed is rewarding to him. The next time his sensory system is challenged, he will be likely to demonstrate verbal aggression again, because it worked the first time. A more effective response would be to tell the child that it is not okay to call people names, and help him make a choice on the playground that will work for him.

Promote Self-Awareness

Part of the learning process as a teacher includes gaining an understanding of the effect of certain sensory inputs on children. Help the child identify environmental issues that are over-stimulating. If Connor gets angry and pushes other children while dancing to music, take a moment to reflect on his behavior. You may recognize that the volume or type of music is over-stimulating to him. He acts as a Sensory Avoider and tries to get away from the music by pushing other children. Take time to assist Connor in recognizing his feelings and the connection to the sensation. For example, you could firmly respond to Connor, "We don't push. It seems like the music is too loud for you. You should ask, 'Would you please turn down the music?'"

You should also help children who are Sensory Seekers become aware of their behaviors. Cheyenne constantly puts objects in her mouth, especially during center and circle times. She seeks tactile input through her mouth. When Cheyenne begins to chew on her shirt, you could take her aside and say, "Cheyenne, it seems like you need something in your mouth. It is not okay to chew your shirt. Let's get some raisins for you to eat." This gives Cheyenne something appropriate to chew on, rather than her shirt. It also helps her begin to understand her sensory cravings so that she can look for ways to handle those needs. If you are concerned about caloric intake, try offering sugar-free gum or chewy snacks.

Respect the Child's Emotions

Respect a child's fears and responses that appear extreme. It is common for children to demonstrate behaviors that look like stubbornness or anger in reaction to sensory information that is over-stimulating for them. Before reading this book, you may have thought it would be most appropriate to help a child by making him interact or try an activity. As you begin to consider the child's sensory integration, you now understand that this may not be a useful approach. The child who is responding in this manner may be sending the signal, "I'm afraid" or "That hurts." Do not force the Sensory Avoider to touch or participate in an activity that his sensory system finds overwhelming. Instead, the most appropriate response would be to gently encourage the child and allow him to watch first and experience later.

Trust a child's need for more sensory input. The Sensory Seeker who is constantly moving sends the signal that he needs more vestibular input. For instance, the child may get up and wander around the room during circle time. The least successful response to this behavior would be to take away movement opportunities by putting him in time out or restricting outside playtime. This type of punishment will eventually increase the negative behavior in the learning environment. Instead, provide the child with regular intervals of movement experiences throughout the day, which can resemble "movement breaks," or by providing a cushion to wiggle on while sitting. This method assists the child in maintaining focus during quiet activities that require more attention.

Provide Consistency

It is important to maintain a consistent environment for preschoolers. This includes choosing a reliable, positive approach to discipline. Responses to all children should be based on each child's individual needs, whether the child has SPD or processes sensations effectively.

Provide positive feedback when the child learns how to manage his sensory needs, which shows the child that you have noticed his growing ability to take care of himself. In the future, the child will be more likely to take care of his own sensory needs rather than have you solve the problem for him.

Do not force the Sensory Avoider to touch or participate in an activity that his or her sensory system finds overwhelming.

Lee is in the Music Center. He adjusts the volume level on the CD player. You could say, "Lee, I noticed that you turned down the music volume to enjoy it more. That was a great idea!"

It takes time to see the benefits of environmental practices. Sometimes, the behaviors will get worse before they get better. Just keep doing what you are doing. If you decide to modify the environment, try it for at least two weeks before determining its usefulness. Be consistent in the approach and carefully evaluate the results of changes. Then, make additional changes that will improve the children's learning environment.

Visual Environment

The way the environment looks to a young child is very important. The classroom could be visually overwhelming and distracting for children who have SPD. When designing the visual environment, consider the child's perspective. Remember that they are little people. One way to see from their point of view is to take a picture of the classroom while kneeling. Then, assess the view. What does it look like? What is on the walls? What is hanging from the ceiling? What is sitting on the floor? What is under the tables and on the shelves? Does it look inviting? Does it look safe? Is there too much visual input?

Encourage a Child's Sense of Space

A well-designed environment helps young children feel secure. If a child feels comfortable in the learning environment, he will be less likely to show signs of oversensitivity to sensory inputs. One way to make the environment appear safe and inviting is to include child-size furniture and tools. Place objects and materials at their eye level, so the children get the sense that this is their space. Place storage containers with materials for the children to use at a reachable height to decrease the chance of knocking over a container and getting injured. Label items so children can be independent and make their own decisions.

Take care to make the space aesthetically beautiful by including items, such as plants, rugs, floor lighting, pillows, and window coverings that make the room attractive. Young children feel safe, secure, and in control in an environment that is beautiful, organized, and encourages active involvement with materials in the learning space.

Use Proper Lighting

Lighting has a significant influence on the atmosphere of the classroom. Most preschool classrooms have too much artificial light. Fluorescent lighting can be visually uncomfortable and over-stimulating for a child with Sensory Processing Disorder (SPD). Exchange cool white tubes, which are usually found in early childhood classrooms, for warm light or full-spectrum tubes. Full-spectrum lighting provides more natural light, which is more comfortable to children's eyes.

It is desirable to have both light and darker spaces in the environment. For example, you may want more direct light in the Art Center so that children can see the materials. Low lighting in the Private Space Center can be relaxing and calming for children with SPD. Incandescent area lamps are softer and less intense than fluorescent lighting. These may be used in the Home Living Center to simulate a home-like environment. Dimmer switches are a nice option for areas of the room used for different activities, such as circle time and rest time. Clip-on lights can provide additional variations by focusing light on a particular area.

Glare from natural light can be visually over-stimulating for children with SPD. Natural light may be controlled with a variety of window coverings to prevent glare. These can include blinds, shades, or curtains.

Organize the Classroom

A well-designed preschool classroom considers young children's developing sense of vision and proprioception (body position). Often, young preschoolers are not as aware of their bodies and how to move them as older preschoolers. Young preschoolers' depth perception, an important component of vision, has not finished developing. As a result, young preschoolers bump into each other more often and receive more minor injuries from falls than older preschoolers. Even older preschoolers do not have fully developed senses of vision and proprioception.

Clear traffic patterns help young children move around the classroom with ease. It is important for the young child to be able to see and recognize where activities are set up in their space. Unique and separate areas communicate clearly what happens in the space, how the materials are used, and the behaviors that can occur. If the path between areas is clearly identified, the young child who is visually oversensitive or who lacks good proprioception will know where to go. For example, when a child enters the room, there is an area for entry materials, which could include clothing storage and a sign-in sheet. He understands easily what happens in the entry area—he puts away his clothes and signs in.

Upon entering, the child decides where to go. After surveying the possibilities, he might choose to go to the Block Center. If the path is designed effectively, he can see and move to that area without distractions or equipment in the way. A bookcase, lattice, or low wall helps to establish the traffic flow pattern so that children move easily from one area to another.

Reduce Clutter

Many early childhood classrooms are filled with clutter. Often, this is the result of a lack of ample storage space and containers. Teachers also keep materials out in the classroom because they never know when the materials will be needed, and the clutter problem grows when there is little time to store and re-shelve. A cluttered landscape is visually over-stimulating for children with SPD. These children are unable to focus on tasks because their visual attention is drawn to the clutter rather than the activity.

The first step in reducing clutter is to assess your classroom needs. Focus on one area of the room at a time. What do you use? What do you need to store? Can the children find the items? Downsizing materials will allow for better use of existing storage, and more is not always better. If an item has not been used in two years, it is not likely to be used—reassess its use, recycle it, or give it away. Once you determine what to keep, decide how to store the materials. Store materials close to where they are going to be used. Sand play items, such as shovels, strainers, buckets, and molds should be stored close to the sand and water table, so that the children can reach them easily.

Clear storage units work best because everyone can see what is inside. Label the container to make it easy to identify. Find ways to display materials attractively and keep them organized. Be creative in your storage selections. Try baskets, pottery pieces, decorative boxes, cans, and shoeboxes. Group items together that are used for similar purposes.

Clutter Management

1. You won't use it if you don't see it.
2. Keep things where you need them.
3. Everything has a place.
4. Label storage places clearly.
5. If it has not been used in two years, it is not going to be used.

Display Children's Work

Consider the function of the display. What do you want people to see? How can it be presented in a clear, organized, and attractive manner? If the display is informational, such as parent notices, menus, center schedules, or activities, it would be more appropriately placed at adult eye level. Post this type of display outside the classroom, on the door, or in the hallway. This placement will decrease visual over-stimulation in the classroom for children with SPD.

Use the children's artwork to celebrate the learning that occurs. Limit your display to items that were most recently completed. Alternate examples so that each child has their work displayed, but not too many at one time.

When displaying art or photographs, use a simple background that will not be distracting. Remember that neutral, solid-color backgrounds are best for great works of art. Think about the color of the background, as well. Bright, bold colors may overshadow the children's work. Use bookcases to display children's larger work. Keeping displays of artwork simple and organized is a must to decrease visual over-stimulation.

Document Progress

Documentation helps parents and other visitors identify the learning that occurs as children participate in any activity. When documenting an ongoing project or other activity, select a few pictures with key phrases for display in the classroom. Documentation should show the children's work on projects throughout the process. For instance, if the class is working on a project related to bird nests, include photographs of the children involved in each step of the study. This may include exploring nests initially, reading books related to nests, collecting materials to make nests, and making bird nests. Use the documentation board to include the actual words that the children used during each stage of the process.

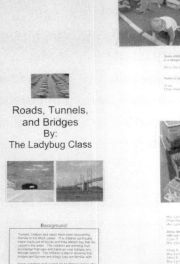

Provide Personal Space

Young children's environment must be responsive to their interests and include items that are meaningful to them. Children enjoy collecting familiar and favorite objects, and they like to keep those things close to them. Give young children a place to store their special things. By doing so, children can help themselves receive the sensory stimulation they need at a specific moment. For instance, a child may need to get his stuffed bunny out of his cubby to give it a firm hug before he can transition to the playground.

Auditory Environment

The early childhood environment contains many types of auditory (sound) stimuli, including, but not limited to, voices of children and adults, music, banging of objects, electronic toys, and running water. Spaces filled with too much noise are overwhelming to some young children. Constant loud sounds may desensitize children's hearing and decrease their ability to discriminate between sounds.

Quiet spaces that are separated from loud areas offer an escape from over-stimulating auditory input. Children who attempt to avoid loud noises may hide under tables or in corners or cover their ears. Children

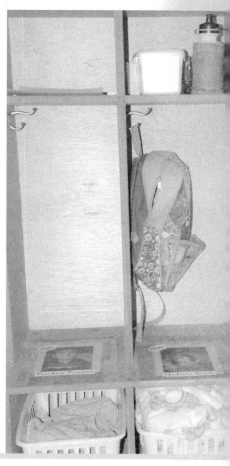

If you can give each child a sense of control over his or her sensory input, he or she will be able to tolerate the sensation better.

who are over-sensitive to certain sounds will be distracted and unable to focus on other important classroom activities.

Hard surfaces, such as tile floors, concrete blocks, and wooden furniture reflect the intensity of sound. A variety of materials and techniques can soften sounds or confine loud activities to certain areas of the classroom. For instance, soft surfaces, such as carpet, fabric, and perforated ceiling tiles absorb sound and decrease reverberations. Adding cushioned furniture, pillows, and sound panels (see Chapter 6 for instructions) absorbs sounds in a noisy early childhood environment. All these methods will help decrease auditory over-stimulation.

A quiet space or learning center may be designed in the classroom to give children a safe place to go when they are overwhelmed by auditory input. The quiet space may be a cardboard box, tent, or partially closed area. It should have soft materials, such as a beanbag chair, blankets, and pillows, to soak up sound. Earphones and quiet, rhythmic music or a white noise machine may drown out other noises. Young children may use this area to focus and prepare to re-enter the activities of the classroom.

Music stimulates brain development in young children, particularly visual, movement, and language skills. It is important to include music in the early childhood environment. However, be careful to adjust the volume appropriately for those children with auditory processing problems. Consider both the intensity of the sound and the rhythm of the music—both have an impact on a child's auditory system. Music with a steady beat and tempo, such as marches and some pop and folk music, assists in making a child feel alert and focused. Music that has a changing rhythm or tempo, such as jazz music, may be confusing and over-stimulating. Using soft, rhythmic music calms young children and is best to use during rest time. If you can give each child a sense of control over his sensory input, he will be able to tolerate the sensation better. Some children cannot tolerate background music and are overwhelmed by it. However, they may enjoy participating in singing a song. It is important to carefully observe the impact of music on the individual child who has SPD to determine how long and when to play music.

Tactile (Touch) Environment

A preschool classroom's tactile environment includes a wide range of materials, textures, objects, and touches. In this active learning space, exploring new materials is commonplace. Touch helps preschoolers develop their cognitive, motor, and social-emotional skills. Through the sense of touch, a young child has the opportunity to learn beginning math and science concepts as well as new vocabulary words and language. Touch is also one method that teachers use to make a child feel safe and secure in the classroom. Teachers hold preschoolers' hands, pat their backs, and hug them to demonstrate affection and love.

Keep in mind that every child is an individual. Different children want different amounts and types of touch input. For example, a child who is a Tactile Avoider may not want to be hugged or to interact with new tactile experiences. This child may turn his back when the teacher tries to hug him or may refuse to participate in some classroom activities. Other preschoolers who are Tactile Seekers may seem to want too much touch input. They may hang on to the teacher throughout the day or get overly messy. Providing a classroom with opportunities to explore and interact with a variety of textures using different approaches is necessary to meet the learning needs of all preschoolers.

Use a variety of materials to add texture to the classroom environment. Soft materials, rugs, and pillows help the classroom feel like home. Select pillows made from a variety of sturdy and washable fabrics, such as denim, corduroy, and cotton. Children love to play on the floor. Placing carpet or rugs on the floor makes the area more comfortable for building with blocks, putting babies to sleep, or sitting during circle time. Choose rugs that are attractive, have an interesting texture, and are safe for walking. Do not select rugs that have complex patterns or letters of the alphabet because these can be visually distracting.

Children who are Sensory Seekers will enjoy art that is touchable. Sensory Under-Responders need opportunities to touch and interact with the environment. Preschoolers can help in making a textured collage to hang on a wall. Begin by selecting a variety of scrap materials with many different textures. The children can cut the pieces and paste them onto a large piece of butcher paper. Be sure to label the different

Children love to play on the floor. Placing carpet or rugs on the floor makes the area more comfortable for building with blocks, putting babies to sleep, or sitting during circle time.

textures. You can use words such as *soft, smooth,* and *rough,* or label the fabric by name, such as *satin, silk,* and so on. This collage can act as a "feely wall" for the children to touch.

Use Firm Touches

The type of touch input given to a child is extremely important. A young child's sense of touch discrimination is not fully developed. In most cases, their brain is not ready to tell the difference between the touch of a feather and the touch of a cotton ball when their eyes are closed. Children's brains can understand firm touch easier than light touch.

When you pat or hug a child firmly you are giving him a firm touch. This type of touch is comforting and soothing. Most children prefer that you massage or firmly pat their backs at nap time, rather than lightly scratch or tickle them. In fact, a young child's brain will sometimes register a light touch as pain rather than pleasant touch input. While people enjoy massage because it relaxes their bodies and makes them feel better, they do not necessarily enjoy getting "lightly tickled."

Introducing Touch Input

Be sure to consider how a young child's temperament influences his interest level in tactile experiences. For instance, a child who is slow to warm up may need extra time and more detailed explanations before he is willing to touch the snow-like material that is in the sand and water table, while the easygoing child may be the first to put his hands in the new or unusual material. Using a consistent approach to introducing new tactile experiences to your preschoolers benefits all children.

"Look first, touch later" is a good rule of thumb for introducing new textures to young children. A child who is a Sensory Avoider or a Sensory Under-Responder and is initially uninterested in a certain texture may want to touch the texture at a later time. Begin by giving a simple description of the activity to the children, "Today, we are going to use glue and sand to make pictures." Ask the children who jumped right into the experience to describe how the material feels: "Ling, is the sand rough or smooth?" "Anna, what does the papier-mâché feel like?" Next, help the child who does not want to participate right away feel as secure as possible. You might say, "It's okay if you want to watch. You can touch it when you are ready." This will take some pressure off the child and let him see that you understand how he feels. In addition, the option gives the child a sense of control. He may touch the material that day or it may take him three or four more times before he is ready.

When introducing a new texture to a child who is afraid or unsure, do not force him to touch the material. Forcing a child to touch a texture or material makes the child feel that he has no control over his environment. Taking away a child's freedom to explore the surroundings will be detrimental to his self-esteem. Instead, gently encourage the child to participate. Better yet, make it so much fun that he really wants to join in. Then, be patient. The child will participate in his own time. As with most of the other sensory inputs, children will tolerate touching more textures and materials if they control the input.

"I Touch" Center

To address the needs of all children, you can offer learning centers that are open ended. A well-designed center allows Sensory Seekers the opportunity to feel and touch a variety of materials and textures and provides the Sensory Avoiders the ability to make choices as to what they feel comfortable touching. An example of a center that will meet these diverse individual tactile needs is the "I Touch" Center. This center offers young children experiences that develop their sense of touch by providing unique textures and materials. It can also guide children to self-awareness and a greater understanding of how to meet their own tactile needs.

> **Forcing a child to touch a texture or material makes the child feel that he or she has no control over his or her environment.**

Teacher- and Parent-Collected Props for the "I Touch" Center:

❖ fabric scraps, such as fur, satin, lace, leather, cotton, wool, denim, and corduroy
❖ cooking supplies, such as cornstarch and flour
❖ household materials, such as cotton balls, foil, plastic wrap, and yarn
❖ glue and scissors
❖ construction paper
❖ broom and dust pan or small vacuum
❖ sand and water table or plastic containers on the floor
❖ shower curtain or plastic to cover the floor
❖ playdough
❖ stuffed animals

Remember that it is okay for a child to look first and touch later. Do not force a child to touch or feel a texture. Introduce the "I Touch" Center to the children and guide their interactions by having fun in your explorations and modeling playful behavior. Observe their involvement and take notes of individual responses such as the child's like or dislike of certain textures for future reference.

Help for Picky Eaters

Many preschoolers who have SPDs are picky eaters. Food preferences vary from child to child. One child might eat only fruits and meats. Another might eat only fried foods. Still another child might eat only bread and cheese. Many things impact the eating patterns of young children, including parental modeling, socioeconomic level, religion, and schedule/timing among others. Often, we forget to think about the effect of young children's sensory processing system and developmental levels on their eating habits.

Preschoolers like their routines, and they are creatures of habit. By nature, it is hard for a preschooler to try a new food that he has never seen or been offered. On average, a young child will have a new food placed on his plate 20 times before he will eat it. So, keep placing the food item on the preschooler's plate. Eventually, he may actually taste it or eat it.

Young children also like to touch before they taste. Allow preschoolers to explore new foods. Add the study of one food each week into the curriculum. For instance, this week, study broccoli, read books about growing vegetables, weigh broccoli, talk about the texture and color of the broccoli, and complete a chart of all the children who "like broccoli" or "do not like broccoli" during center time. Placing raw broccoli in the Garden Center or Home Living Center also provides preschoolers with opportunities to explore the food item. Integrated activities such as these allow preschoolers to become more comfortable with the food item before they have it on their plates.

Vestibular (Movement and Balance) Environment

Some children search for challenging movement opportunities within and outside the classroom while other children are more cautious and refuse to participate in some motor activities. A wide range of movement experiences should be available to meet the vestibular needs of all children. There are children who are afraid to do any activity requiring their feet to leave the ground, such as swinging or climbing. Therefore, it is helpful to have movement opportunities that do not involve the children's feet off the ground for very long. This may include running, hopping, jumping rope, rolling, playing with a parachute, and games like Simon Says.

Rotating Activity Level

Preschoolers are active learners. They learn through moving and exploring their concrete environment. Typical preschoolers can sit quietly for a maximum of 15 minutes. After that time, they start moving, wiggling, squirming, putting their hands on their neighbors, and so on.

When you ask a preschooler to sit for too long, it leads to inappropriate behaviors and loss of attention. The schedule for the day should include a rotation between active and quiet learning opportunities.

Sample Daily Routine

8:00–8:30	Welcome – Free Choice	Active
8:30–9:00	Small Motor or Journal Writing	Quiet
9:00–9:20	Morning Circle Time	Quiet
9:20–9:40	Snack/Bathroom	
9:40–10:40	Center Time	Active
10:40–11:00	Regroup with Circle Time	Quiet
11:00–11:30	Outdoor/Indoor Motor Play	Active
11:30–12:00	Lunch/Bathroom	
12:00–2:00	Rest	Quiet
2:00–2:20	Snack/Bathroom	
2:20–3:20	Center Time	Active
3:20–3:40	Reflection/Closing	Quiet
3:40–5:00	Outside Play	Active

Alternating quiet and active times gives preschoolers vital opportunities for vestibular input. Children who are Vestibular Seekers need more intense large-motor opportunities throughout the day. When a Vestibular Seeker receives an adequate amount of vestibular input, he can be more attentive during quiet periods, such as circle time and teacher-directed activities.

All preschoolers learn through movement and interaction with the world; it is best to give them regular intervals of active time throughout the day. But, children who are Vestibular Avoiders or Under-Responders will need gentle encouragement to participate in large movement experiences.

One way to provide motor opportunities to meet the vestibular needs of all children is to set up a Gross Motor Center in the classroom. An indoor Gross Motor Center provides children with the opportunity to select the types of movement input they need. It will also help them learn about and control their bodies.

Gross Motor Center

Teacher- and Parent-Collected Props for the Gross Motor Center:

❖ floor mat or plush carpet
❖ soft balls of all sizes
❖ balance beam
❖ unbreakable mirror
❖ blankets
❖ cardboard boxes
❖ hula hoops
❖ child-size rocking chair
❖ carpet rolls (see Chapter 6 for instructions)

The Gross Motor Center will facilitate young children's large motor development, including strength, coordination, balance, and flexibility. The center also gives young children a positive method of receiving vestibular input.

Proprioception (Body Position) Environment

The proprioceptive sense tells the body what the muscles, joints and body parts are doing and in what position. A child needs a well-functioning proprioceptive sense and tactile sense to have adequate body awareness. Proprioception impacts coordination and timing of movements. It is important for preschool teachers to include activities that facilitate body awareness in young children, as it influences

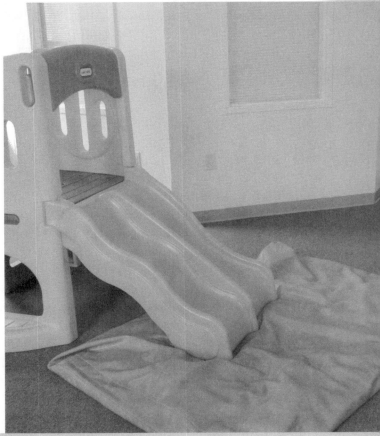

not only the children's skill level in large motor activities, such as catching a ball and running, but also in small motor activities, such as handwriting and cutting with scissors.

A child who has underdeveloped proprioception will have difficulty with everyday preschool motor activities, such as walking, climbing stairs, running, and jumping. A child with poorly developed body awareness may also have poor handwriting and experience difficulty in manipulating small objects, such as stringing beads or stacking small blocks.

Heavy Work Activities

Offering preschoolers heavy work activities throughout the day will help promote their sense of body position. For many children, participating in heavy work activities organizes their minds, helps them maintain their attention, and has a positive impact on their focus during classroom activities.

One way to make an activity heavy work for a preschooler is to add resistance. Choose materials for art activities that are harder to manipulate, such as finger paint, clay, or foam soap. For drawing activities, have the child draw with chalk on sandpaper or write in sand. Provide crayons or pencils, which take more pressure to draw with than markers. Add texture to the drawing surface or the writing utensil. This makes the fingers work a little bit more and sends more signals from the fingers to the child's brain, which enhances proprioception.

Another simple way to increase the workload of an activity is to use vertical surfaces for art and drawing. This may include having children draw on chalkboards or easels, or you can also tape paper to the wall for painting. Make or purchase incline boards (see Chapter 6 for instructions) to sit on tables or the floor for a different writing or drawing surface. Vertical surfaces facilitate the child's use of his entire arm for drawing or writing, which is heavy work for the child.

Preschoolers can participate in many fun activities that are innately heavy work. Almost any activity that occurs on an outdoor play structure is hard work, including climbing, jumping, and swinging. Other large motor activities, such as rolling, hopping, skipping, throwing and catching balls, digging in the sand, and using riding toys, also include resistance and increase proprioception.

Remember that some of these activities can be used inside as well as outside and may help preschoolers organize their minds and stay alert. It is particularly useful to have a young child participate in a heavy work activity immediately before a quiet activity. For instance, you could have the children "march," stomping their feet firmly, to marching band music on their way to circle time.

All preschool children can benefit from a classroom that is designed with careful consideration of children's sensory processing needs. Simple modifications to the classroom, such as changing the light bulbs or adding a picture schedule, can dramatically improve young children's daily involvement in the classroom. The next chapter will guide you in using your developing awareness of sensory processing skills to address the needs of individual preschoolers who have sensory processing disorders.

Help for Preschoolers with Sensory Processing Disorder

CHAPTER 4

Modifying the Environment

As you develop a greater understanding of young children's sensory integration skills, you will notice that most preschoolers have at least a minor problem in one sensory area (visual, auditory, tactile, vestibular, or proprioceptive). Some preschoolers may have significant difficulties in at least one sensory area. If the problem has a negative impact on their daily lives, they may be diagnosed with Sensory Processing Disorder (SPD). The child who has SPD will be unable to participate and learn effectively in the preschool environment. Whether the child is ultimately diagnosed with SPD or has only a few mild sensory issues, you should make modifications to the preschool environment.

The purpose of a sensory diet is to assist the child in functioning better within his or her world.

The information that follows provides some easy-to-use methods to help make the young child's time in your preschool classroom more positive, effective, and appropriate. All of these recommendations require direct supervision by an adult. Special consideration for each child's specific sensory needs is a must; not every suggestion will work with every child, and some of the methods or modifications may be too challenging for some children. Discuss these suggestions with the child's occupational therapist and parents before implementing any of them.

It can take several weeks or months to see changes in a child following modifications to the environment. You may want to change only one thing at a time; if too many changes are made in the environment, it will be difficult to determine what is making a difference for the child. Re-assess the child's classroom performance after two or three weeks. Do you see changes in the child's responses to sensory input? Do you see changes in the child's behaviors? If you do not see improvement, try a different modification. If you still do not see a positive change, then contact the child's therapist and parents.

Sensory Diet

A sensory diet is an activity program that a therapist develops to meet the sensory needs of an individual child with SPD. The purpose of a sensory diet is to assist the child in functioning better within her world. A therapist will specifically design activities to help the child be more focused and skillful in everyday tasks (Wilbarger & Wilbarger, 1991).

A child in your classroom who is receiving occupational therapy to address sensory processing problems may also be provided with a sensory diet. Sensory Seekers need more input than most children and they will attempt to get it any way that they can. Sensory Under-Responders need input too, but they do not know how to get that input. The sensory diet includes tactile (touch), vestibular (movement and balance), and/or proprioceptive (body position) activities. The sensory diet provides the sensory input that a child craves or the sensory input that a child needs in the most appropriate manner. A sensory diet may also incorporate activities to calm the child or help her focus.

Case Study: Riley

Riley is a four-year-old boy who has a diagnosis of developmental delay. He attends a public school preschool program. Riley is a Sensory Seeker who is constantly bumping into other children, running into walls, and falling on the floor. He falls out of his chair during lunch at least once a day. He is a very messy eater and stuffs his mouth full of food. Riley rolls around the floor during circle and nap time. While he has not established a good relationship with his peers, Riley is a very loving child who gives big hugs to his teacher and tries to hug the other children. He is particularly rough with other boys whom he tries to tackle on the playground.

The occupational therapist (OT) working for the school system collaborated with Riley's teacher to prepare a sensory diet for him to use at preschool. The diet is aimed at giving Riley the sensory input he seeks, and it uses many heavy work principles to help Riley through appropriate activities spread throughout his day.

Sample Sensory Diet for Riley

The following activities are designed to help Riley through heavy work activities. These methods should help decrease Riley's inappropriate sensory seeking behaviors, such as bumping into other children and rolling around on the floor. The activities work most effectively by using one or two each day. Alternate the heavy work that Riley uses, so that his sensory system does not get bored with the techniques and stop working. In three months, we (OT and teacher) will reassess Riley's needs and change the sensory diet, as indicated.

Sensory Diet for Riley:

❖ Add weight to Riley's backpack by placing several hardcover books inside. Riley should wear his backpack (over both shoulders) from the car into the preschool.

❖ Give Riley the official "Mr. Clean" classroom job. This classroom duty can include wiping down tables, pushing up chairs to tables, or vacuuming the floor.

❖ Prior to circle time, snack time, or lunch time (any time he needs to sit still), have Riley march around the room, hop like a bunny, crawl like a lion, or stomp like an elephant.

❖ During circle time, snack time, or lunch time (any time he needs to sit still), give Riley a sand pillow (see Chapter 6 for instructions) to place in his lap.

❖ Place a mini-trampoline in the Gross Motor Center. Allow Riley to jump for five minutes each hour.

❖ Let Riley help you stock the Library Center shelves or carry books from the school library to the classroom.

❖ Place a crash pad (see Chapter 6 for instructions) in the Gross Motor Center for Riley to crash into or roll around on.

❖ Give Riley chewy foods to eat at lunch and snack. Examples of healthy chewy foods include bagels, dried fruit, cheese sticks, and fruit chews.

❖ Let Riley pull two other preschoolers around in a big wagon to and from the lunch room or playground.

❖ Roll Riley in a large quilt (like a burrito) for rest time.

Good sensory diets are planned with careful consideration for the preschool environment. As the child's teacher, your input concerning a child's sensory needs is valuable. Collaborating with the child's parents and therapist is the key to an effective sensory diet. The child's sensory diet will need to be modified occasionally. If you do not adjust the child's sensory diet, the child may adapt to the sensory inputs and the diet will no longer be effective. Regular communication between the teacher and parents assists in making updates or changes in the sensory diet, as needed.

Calming and Organizing Activities

Calming and organizing activities help children decrease over-stimulation from sensory inputs. These activities are most useful for Sensory Avoiders who are easily overwhelmed by certain sensations. However, they may be used in the classroom to help all children become more focused and ready to learn. These activities help prevent over-stimulation in preschoolers, and can help you respond to negative behaviors that young children may use to avoid sensory input, such as physical aggression, verbal aggression, crying, or hiding.

Calming and organizing activities include the following:

❖ heavy work activities, such as jumping, rolling, climbing, pushing and pulling objects, animal walks, and catching and throwing a heavy ball

❖ eating chewy foods, such as dried fruit, granola bars, cheese sticks or blocks, bagels, or chewing gum

❖ listening to Baroque or other rhythmic music

❖ using a picture schedule (see Chapter 6 for instructions) of the typical daily schedule

❖ drinking thick liquids through a straw

❖ rocking in a rocking chair or swinging

❖ firm rubbing of the back or "bear hugs"

❖ smelling a calming scent, such as vanilla

Alerting Activities

Alerting activities are used to assist young children who are under-stimulated by sensory inputs. These activities are appropriate for children who need more sensory input to remain alert and aware of their surroundings. It is most beneficial to use these activities in response to

preschoolers who appear sleepy, lethargic, or disinterested. They may also be utilized to prevent children from becoming inattentive.

Alerting activities include the following:

❖ movement with or without music
❖ eating crunchy foods, such as raw vegetables, pretzels, crackers, or popcorn
❖ drinking cold beverages or eating cold or spicy foods, such as Popsicles or salsa
❖ bouncing on a large exercise ball
❖ smelling an alerting scent, such as peppermint
❖ jumping on a trampoline

Suggestions for Preschoolers Who Have Visual Processing Problems

Young children who have visual processing problems have difficulty making sense of visual information. This may cause them to seek out more visual input, avoid visual input, or not respond to visual input. If these children are going to reach their learning potential, they will need modification of the visual environment. Children who have visual processing problems must receive the right type and amount of visual input, so they can focus on learning. Modification of the environment may include lighting changes, decreasing the amount of decoration in the classroom, and providing the child with more appropriate visual stimulation.

Visual Avoiders

Visual Avoiders overreact to visual input, such as cluttered environments, high contrasts (black and white), bright lights, and flickering lights. Some visual inputs will be painful for the Visual Avoider and cause her to close her eyes or look away. To help the child maintain visual attention, allow her to wear sunglasses inside and outside the classroom. Some children may prefer to wear a hat or visor. These techniques reduce glare on the child's eyes.

Modify the classroom environment by decreasing visual inputs. Reducing bright lighting, such as fluorescent lights, in the classroom has an overall calming effect on Visual Avoiders. Floor and table lamps, instead of overhead lighting, are less visually overwhelming for all children. Use a sheet or fabric to cover open shelves and decrease visual distraction from toys or objects.

Decrease clutter and high visual contrasts in the Visual Avoider's workspace. For example, instead of having the child's name taped to the top of her table, give her a clean space to work, and cover her workspace with plain, pastel-colored paper to decrease glare and visual contrast. A blank piece of paper for drawing or writing is easiest for the child to manage. Give the child frequent eye rest breaks by allowing her to close her eyes every few minutes while she works on visually taxing activities.

Visual Seekers

The Visual Seeker seems to crave more visual input than the average preschooler. She may stare at a flickering fluorescent light or stand at the window rubbing her fingers across the blinds repeatedly.

Preventing staring behaviors or obsessions with visual input is the best option. Satisfy the child's visual craving by adding extra visual inputs to her daily routine. This may be accomplished through a sensory diet that gives the child her fill of visual stimulation, so she can focus on other classroom activities. For instance, provide a flashlight with color lighting options for the child to use during play. Then, in circle time, she may be able to focus on you and the calendar, rather than the fluorescent lights.

Visual Under-Responders

Preschoolers who are Under-Responders to visual information need plenty of opportunities to develop their sense of vision. This child will need your encouragement to participate in developmentally appropriate visual experiences such as drawing, painting, gluing, cutting, writing, and looking at books or other print materials. Always seek the child's direct eye contact before making a request. Use positive and direct statements such as, "Callie, come on over and paint with us!"

Consider ways to facilitate appropriate visual input while also promoting the social skills that Under-Responders often lack. Select a child who is particularly adept at social interactions and who can guide the child who is under-responsive. Ask this preschooler to be the Under-Responder's "buddy" or "helper." Then encourage the pair to work on projects together.

The processing of auditory information is very important for life skills, such as language, social and emotional skills, and cognitive skills.

Suggestions for Preschoolers with Auditory Processing Problems

Preschoolers who have problems with auditory processing are able to hear, but their brains process sounds incorrectly or inadequately. Everyday noises may be overwhelming for some of these children, while others consistently seek loud sounds and noises. Some children with auditory problems appear not to hear certain sounds or noises, particularly when these sounds are continuous, such as background music. The processing of auditory information is very important for life skills, such as language, social and emotional skills, and cognitive skills. Simple adaptations to the preschool environment can make a significant impact on these children's development.

Auditory Avoiders

Easily over-stimulated by auditory information, the Auditory Avoider may avoid sounds by placing her hands over her ears, hiding, or running away. Certain sounds, such as an alarm or vacuum cleaner, may actually be painful to this child. If you know that a disturbing noise will occur in the classroom, such as the school bell at the end of the day, it is best to prepare the child beforehand by saying, "Myra, in two minutes, the bell will ring." Then, allow the child to go to a quiet place, such as the Private Place Center or the bathroom, to get away from the sound.

Many Auditory Avoiders are particularly sensitive to crowd noise. In the classroom, the noise level may increase substantially during center time. During loud periods, it may help the child to wear earplugs, headphones,

or ear muffs. The child will still hear direct conversations, but the overall noise level will be toned down. The child should not wear earplugs for the entire day or her ears will accommodate to the sound and the earplugs will no longer work, and even soft sounds may begin to over-stimulate the child.

Soak up sound in the classroom by using rugs, carpet, pillows, and fabric. Sounds, such as humming of the fluorescent lights, bubbling of the fish tank, and buzzing of the air conditioner, may be auditory distracters for the child; consider seating the child away from these sounds. Place the child at a table away from the door or window. Noises from the hallway or playground may draw the child's attention away from classroom activities. Do not speak loudly in the classroom. Remember, this may hurt her ears.

Allowing the child access to a favorite comfort object, such as a stuffed animal or blanket, may be useful. The Auditory Avoider may need to use this comfort object to soothe herself. Try giving the child a firm bear hug to help organize her brain; allow her time to regain her composure and re-enter classroom activities when she is ready.

Auditory Seekers

An Auditory Seeker thrives in noisy situations and craves excessive auditory input. This child likes to turn the volume up, up, up! She may even hold the speaker next to her ear. The Auditory Seeker may talk and sing loudly and have difficulty using her "inside voice." This child's brain needs more sound and noise input than the typical child. It is best to provide Auditory Seekers with auditory input that will fulfill her needs but will not distract from learning activities.

Provide headphones for use in the Music Center. Encourage the child to use earphones to listen to his favorite music on the playground or during center time. Provide noisy materials for the child to use in the Art Center, including cellophane, newspaper, and bubble wrap. These modifications promote development and provide auditory input. Placing the child in a seat away from the doorway or windows decreases his attention to noises outside the classroom. Make sure the child sits next to you during circle time so that you can help her focus on your voice rather than sounds the other children make.

Auditory Under-Responders

A preschooler who is an Auditory Under-Responder may appear to be unaware of the typical sounds of the classroom. She may respond inconsistently to your requests. If she does reply, her response may be slow and quiet. This child will have particular difficulty attending to your voice when there is constant background noise, such as an air conditioner or quiet, rhythmical music. The Under-Responder will tend to interact more appropriately to sounds when the environment is chaotic. Changes in sounds tend to activate her sensory system to respond.

During morning circle or group activities, it may help to place this child close to you. When you speak to her, try to vary your volume level and use an exclamatory tone of voice. You could also place the Under-Responsive child next to a talkative preschooler who will seek out an appropriate response. When selecting music, choose a mix of slow and fast songs so that the sounds do not become disinteresting for this child.

Suggestions for Preschoolers with Tactile (Touch) Processing Problems

Preschool is full of tactile experiences such as playdough, paint, sand and water, blocks, and Legos. Children may not be able to interact appropriately with tactile materials when their brains do not process this type of information efficiently or appropriately. Some children who have tactile processing problems may show extreme emotions or overreact to common textures or materials found in the preschool classroom. Other children may seem to crave touch experiences by placing objects in their mouths, rubbing textures across their bodies, or getting overly messy. Still other children seem totally unaware of textures and temperatures in their environment. All three types of tactile processing deficits require modification in the preschool environment so that the child's learning needs will be met.

Tactile Avoiders (Tactile Defensiveness)

Tactile Avoidance is probably the most identifiable Sensory Processing Disorder (SPD) in preschoolers. A child who is over responsive to tactile input does not want to get messy and may avoid touching textures, such as glue, fingerpaint, playdough, or sand. She may be an extremely picky eater and very particular about her clothes. The Tactile Avoider does not play well with other children, primarily due to her dislike of light or unexpected touch.

When introducing a texture or messy activity to a Tactile Avoider:

❖ Explain to the child what is going to occur.
❖ Give the child permission to sit and watch.
❖ Model playful interactions with the texture.
❖ Be patient. Do not force the child to touch the material.

One way to help a child who avoids tactile input is by preventing unexpected touches. A child who has tactile defensiveness often strikes out at other children or becomes angry or tearful when walking in line. This is because the child gets unexpected touches from the other children that her brain registers as painful or threatening. Decrease the chance of negative behaviors by allowing the child to be the line leader or to walk at the end of the line. Place the child at the head of the table, rather than beside other children. These methods decrease the risk of unexpected touches from other children.

Tell the child beforehand that a touch is going to occur. For instance, "I am going to help you button your jacket." By doing this, you will help the child anticipate and get her sensory system ready for the touch, rather than surprising her and producing an adverse reaction, such as pushing or running away. When touching this child, use a firm touch, as light touch is irritating to the child who is a Tactile Avoider. This child's brain needs firm touch before it will be registered. Therefore, she may be okay with giving bear hugs to her teacher, but she will not like a light pat.

A child who avoids tactile input will do better when initiating the touch. Give the child a sense of control over the tactile environment by letting her know that she can decide if and when she wants to participate. Allow the Tactile Avoider to watch first and touch later, rather than forcing her to touch.

Introduce one tactile input at a time, as it is more difficult for a child to process two new sensations at the same time. Therefore, do not ask the Tactile Avoider to place her bare feet in fingerpaint and then walk across the sidewalk; this would be over-stimulating for the child with tactile defensiveness. Consider the sensory inputs in the surrounding environment, not just the tactile experience. For the best chance of getting the child to participate in a tactile experience, make the external environment less stimulating. Dim the lights, turn off overhead lighting, or use lamps, and decrease the auditory inputs by turning off music and using quiet voices.

Most Tactile Avoiders have poor self-esteem and limited social skills; they do not like to be near other children, because they are afraid to be touched. This prevents them from building relationships with their peers. To facilitate the child's social development, include information on touch in the curriculum. Begin by talking about the different types of touch, using kid-friendly words such as "warm fuzzies" and "cold pricklies." Explain that everyone does not feel touch the same way; some children do not like to be touched, while others love it. You may decide to incorporate a class rule for touching, such as, "Ask before you touch."

Tactile Seekers

The Tactile Seeker, who looks for tactile sensations, may seem as though she has her hands on everything and everyone. This preschooler may put objects in her mouth and like to rub and manipulate toys and materials. The Tactile Seeker may seem to have no awareness of personal space and may be touching you or hanging on you all day.

Most Tactile Avoiders have poor self-esteem and limited social skills; they do not like to be near other children, because they are afraid to be touched.

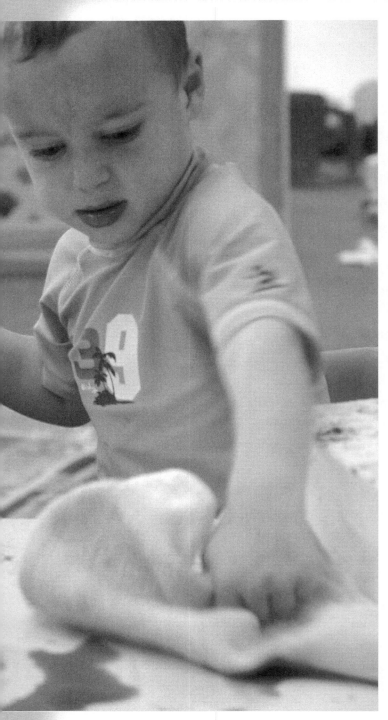

Look for ways to provide appropriate touch sensations. This child may benefit from a sensory diet that includes regular intervals of tactile input throughout the day. For example, rather than toys, you may offer the child some raisins to chew or other chewy food to provide tactile input in her mouth. When the child is seated, provide a textured blanket or pillow to rub, touch, and hold in her lap. This may prevent the child from touching the child next to her. You could use carpet squares during circle time to help the child identify her own space and give her something to touch.

The child who seeks tactile sensations may need a textured object to carry with her during the day. Use a keychain to attach a small toy to her belt loop or place the object in the child's pocket. Some textured items that may be beneficial include a small Koosh ball, twist tie, plastic shower ring, piece of textured fabric, or other small manipulative. Change the item regularly so the child does not become bored with it. If she is not interested in touching the object, it will no longer be a useful tactile input. Establish rules to follow while using the textured item, such as, "The tiny blanket needs to stay in your pocket."

Many preschoolers have difficulty understanding personal space, which is an important concept to follow for good social skills. Young children often get very close to one another when they are talking or almost sit on top of one another at the lunch table. It is particularly challenging for Tactile Seekers to develop an awareness of personal space. Help preschoolers learn about personal space by providing them with physical cues. For example, say, "Spread out your arms really wide. Now, turn around in a circle. That is your personal space." Ask children to stand on a piece of newspaper or inside a hula hoop to give a physical boundary that also acts as personal space, and ask the children to talk to one another from within their personal spaces.

Tactile Under-Responders

A child who is Under-Responsive to touch input will need lots of encouragement to participate in tactile experiences. Take as many opportunities as you can to touch the child. For instance, you can touch the Tactile Under-Responder each time that you speak with her. Pat or rub her back at rest time. Ask her to hold one of her peer's hands on the way to the restroom or out to the playground. Push her on a swing or riding toy. These appropriate touches will help provide her with that tactile input her sensory system needs.

Provide this child with many tactile experiences and then encourage her to interact. Place the Tactile Under-Responder alongside a peer who is creative and social. Then provide activities that will stimulate the child to manipulate tools and materials. Making hand- or footprints on a variety of paper or materials (for example, sandpaper, newspaper, bubble wrap, burlap, or corduroy) can be fun and stimulating for the Under-Responder's tactile sense. Creating sculptures with clay, playdough, foam soap, Styrofoam, or other materials is an open-ended way to promote the tactile sense.

Suggestions for Preschoolers with Vestibular (Movement and Balance) Processing Problems

Children who have vestibular processing problems have difficulty taking in and responding to information about balance, gravity, and movement through space. Many of these children are uncoordinated and fall frequently or have difficulty learning developmentally appropriate motor skills, such as running, climbing, or jumping. They may have poor posture and slump in their seats. Some of these children avoid movement encounters and experience motion sickness easily. Other children with vestibular processing problems need an excessive amount of movement for their brain to make sense of the input, so they appear to be constantly moving around. Vestibular Seekers, Vestibular Avoiders, and Vestibular Under-Responders need a "just-right" quantity of movement input so they can focus on learning activities.

Vestibular Avoiders

Vestibular Avoiders do not enjoy most movement experiences. This child does not like playground equipment and wants to keep her feet on the ground. Instead, she may be found playing in the sand or mulch. She may get carsick easily and need extra time in the morning to feel better before starting the day. The Vestibular Avoider is often clumsy, does not participate in large-motor activities with other children, and may appear lazy because she is afraid to move.

Never force the child to participate in movement experiences that are overwhelming for him or her; let the child be your guide.

Many Vestibular Avoiders display a significant negative physical reaction to too much vestibular input, which is why it is essential for them to receive intervention from an occupational therapist trained in sensory integration. It is important to be aware of some of the signals indicating when a child is reaching her vestibular limit. As with other types of SPD, it is advisable to prevent over-stimulation.

Discontinue the movement activity if you note any of the following signals that a child may be receiving too much vestibular stimulation:

❖ sweating or clamminess

❖ turning pale or blushing

❖ headache

❖ nausea

❖ excitability or excessive giggling

❖ crying

❖ drowsiness

When you are working with a Vestibular Avoider, you must be sure to trust the child's emotions. It is common for them to react with fear or anger when presented with a challenging movement experience. If a preschooler is unwilling to climb the steps to the slide, reassure her that it is okay by saying, "I can see that climbing those stairs is scary for you." Never force the child to participate in movement experiences that are overwhelming for her; let the child be your guide. The child needs to feel safe in her environment before she can try new movement experiences.

A child who avoids vestibular sensations will be more likely to participate in a movement experience that she can control. Providing safe movement opportunities, both inside and outside the classroom, will encourage the child to participate. Do not push the child on the swing unless she asks you to do so. First, gently suggest that the child sit on the swing. With time and encouragement, she will begin to move the swing herself, because she can control the amount of movement and add more when she feels comfortable.

Vestibular Avoiders are often uneasy about activities that take their feet off the ground. Offer movement experiences that allow the child to keep her feet on the ground. For instance, lower an outdoor swing so that her feet touch the ground. Children who are Vestibular Avoiders can tolerate straight, front-and-back, or side-to-side movement before they can cope with diagonal or circular movements. You may experience this when you ride in the back seat of a car, where you feel fine when driving along the interstate, but get queasy when traveling on a winding, mountain road. Sometimes riding toys and push toys feel like safe movement activities for the Vestibular Avoider because they provide straight lines of movement.

Vestibular Seekers

The Vestibular Seeker is always moving—usually at full speed. This child is often considered a "dare devil" who is not afraid to participate in any movement activity. She gets a lot of minor injuries. She has difficulty sitting still. If she is sitting, this child is constantly fidgeting, rocking, or swaying. During center time she quickly moves between the centers, and has trouble participating in socio-dramatic play experiences with her peers, because she does not stay in one place very long.

The Vestibular Seeker has a high sensory threshold. It takes a lot of movement before she gets her fill and is able to sit still. She needs additional vestibular input to help her brain get organized and ready to learn.

Use a sensory diet filled with movement and balance activities to provide the necessary vestibular input. The environment that is best designed for a Vestibular Seeker offers many opportunities for movement inside and outside the classroom. The activities are most effective when provided to the child on a regular basis and spaced throughout the day. Some appropriate movement opportunities for preschoolers include the following:

❖ spinning on a tire swing (see Chapter 6 for instructions) or Sit 'n Spin
❖ balancing or bouncing on a large exercise ball
❖ riding toys, such as tricycles, bicycles, scooters, and Big Wheels
❖ swinging
❖ hula hoops
❖ running and jumping into a crash pad (See Chapter 6 for instructions)
❖ jumping on a mini-trampoline
❖ log rolls or forward flips, especially downhill
❖ playing games like Ring Around the Rosie or The Hokey Pokey

Prevent the child from demonstrating negative vestibular seeking behaviors by alternating active and quiet periods in the daily routine. Instead of doing circle, lunch, and nap in sequence, it is better to insert active times, such as centers, after circle. Provide the child with appropriate movement experiences before asking her to sit still. For example, you may give the Vestibular Seeker the opportunity to twirl around 10 times before sitting for circle time. Prepare the child for transitions to help her settle into the next activity, "In two minutes we will go to circle. You have time to twirl around ten times before you go. I'll help you count!"

Preschoolers are active learners who need to move and interact with their environment so they can learn about the world. Do you have realistic expectations for your preschoolers? Most preschoolers can sit and attend to an activity for a maximum of 15 minutes. Even then, many preschoolers squirm throughout the activity. Consider your goal for the child. Do you want her to learn specific information? Is it absolutely necessary for the child to sit perfectly still? Allow the child the opportunity for movement, within limits. For instance, the child can sit on a soft cushion in a chair. She can then rock back and forth on the cushion as she is listening to instructions. Another option is to let the child stand while she is working on a project. The Vestibular Seeker may benefit from sitting in a child-size rocking chair, in a beanbag chair, or on a pillow during circle. These methods allow the child to focus on the learning activity rather than attempting to get more vestibular input.

Vestibular Under-Responders

The preschool child who is a Vestibular Under-Responder sometimes appears lazy or disinterested in moving in and around the classroom. This child will need focused and changing movement opportunities throughout her daily routine. You will need to guide the Under-

If the child appears especially lethargic or disinterested, you can try using movement to energize him or her.

Responder to participate in the movement activities that she requires for her sensory system to be alert. You may want to pair this child with one of her peers or get all the preschoolers involved in these movement experiences.

It would be especially beneficial for the Vestibular Under-Responder to participate in a movement experience at least once every hour. If the child appears especially lethargic or disinterested, you can try using movement to energize her. Each movement activity does not need to last more than a couple of minutes. Suggestions for the Vestibular Under-Responder include: sitting and bouncing on a large therapy ball, jumping or hopping, swinging outside, spinning on a Sit-N-Spin, twirling around, vigorous dancing, or going down a slide.

Suggestions for Preschoolers with Proprioception (Body Position) Processing Problems

Some preschoolers have difficulty knowing where their bodies are in space. If you ask a child with proprioception problems to close her eyes and hop on one foot, she may not be able to do this because she is unsure of where her legs are without the aid of vision. Children with proprioception processing deficits seem to seek out activities that will give them more input to their muscles and joints. They may crash into walls, hug or lean on their peers, and jump or roll off the playground equipment in search of more proprioceptive input. Other children with proprioception processing problems avoid or just do not seem interested in heavy work activities that require strength. These children sometimes appear lazy because they lie around or do not participate in playground activities or block building. There are several simple solutions for modifying the learning environment that can meet the needs of preschoolers who have proprioception processing problems.

Proprioceptive Avoiders

The child who is a Proprioceptive Avoider does not seem to know what her body is doing. She avoids heavy work, such as cleaning up toys or playing on outdoor equipment. This child may tire easily and appear unmotivated. She may have low muscle tone, poor posture, and poor coordination. She may be unable to walk, dance, climb, or hop as well as the other preschoolers. New motor experiences are very challenging for the Proprioceptive Avoider. When someone tries to help her move her body, she may respond with anger or flight.

A Proprioceptive Avoider benefits from work with an occupational therapist trained in sensory integration. While there are some things teachers can do to assist, this problem area requires a thorough understanding of sensory processing and intervention techniques. Begin by helping the child learn to identify her body parts. Start with the basics: facial features, arms, legs, head, tummy, hands, and feet. Then, progress to more specific parts, such as fingers, toes, elbows, knees, and ankles. Playing games such as Simon Says or singing songs such as "Put Your Finger on Your Nose" and "Head, Shoulders, Knees, and Toes" may help with this process. When interacting with the child, call attention to how she moves her body and what part of her body she uses. You may say, "I see that you are using your fingers to push the paint around in circles."

> **Provide the child with opportunities to use his or her body and participate in motor experiences that provide the just-right challenge.**

Provide the child with opportunities to use her body and participate in motor experiences that provide the just-right challenge. Do not ask the child to complete tasks that she perceives to be very difficult, or she will give up. For instance, if the child cannot hop on two feet, do not ask her to hop on one foot. As the Proprioceptive Avoider is at risk for having low self-esteem, it is essential to provide motor tasks in which she can be successful. Demonstrate how to participate, but do not force or help the child by moving her body. Then, allow the Proprioceptive Avoider extra time to watch and observe motor experiences before she participates. Finally, give positive feedback for her approximations at doing the motor activity. "I really like the way you hopped like a bunny, using both your feet."

Proprioceptive Seekers

The child who is a Proprioceptive Seeker craves forceful movement experiences. This child crashes and bumps into objects and people. She may throw herself onto the floor, push her peers, and jump off furniture

and playground equipment. This child may demonstrate aggressive behaviors, such as kicking, hitting, or biting, to receive the proprioceptive sensations that her body craves.

The Proprioceptive Seeker benefits from opportunities to participate in forceful movement activities. The most appropriate sensory diet for this child would be heavy work and deep pressure activities (see below for specific heavy work activities). Giving the child consistent proprioceptive input throughout the day may help her stay organized and decrease her aggressive-looking behaviors.

Proprioception Under-Responders

Preschoolers who are under-responsive to proprioceptive input do not process body position sensations appropriately. They often appear lazy and may be weak and uncoordinated. These children will benefit from heavy work and deep pressure activities that will stimulate their brain's sensory processing system. But they do not know how to get the proprioceptive input they need. Unlike the Proprioceptive Seeker, the Proprioceptive Under-Responder will require encouragement to participate in these appropriate activities.

Heavy Work Activities

Heavy work activities are designed to give strenuous input to the child's muscles and joints to help the child's brain begin to integrate proprioceptive information effectively. The following heavy work activities are developmentally appropriate for preschoolers:

- ❖ animal walks, such as the crab, snake, elephant, bunny, or duck
- ❖ lifting and carrying heavy loads, such as carrying books to and from the library, moving furniture around the room, or carrying buckets of water on the playground

- ❖ pushing and pulling, such as pulling a wagon full of playground or gym equipment, pushing another child in a stroller or wheelchair, pushing large toy trucks filled with blocks or other heavy objects, and pushing toys through the sand
- ❖ jumping on a mini-trampoline
- ❖ opening heavy doors
- ❖ jumping into a crash pad (See Chapter 6 for instructions)
- ❖ hanging or swinging from the monkey bars
- ❖ standing push-ups against a wall
- ❖ gross motor activities, such as stomping, kicking, catching and throwing heavy balls, jumping, and rolling down a hill
- ❖ eating chewy or crunchy foods
- ❖ playing with materials that are firm, such as modeling clay, putty, and playdough
- ❖ using scissors to cut thick paper, such as construction paper, poster board, or cardstock
- ❖ walking around in or moving inside a body sock (See Chapter 6 for instructions)

Deep Pressure Activities

Deep pressure activities are designed to give firm touch input to promote better integration of tactile information and body positioning. The following deep pressure activities are developmentally appropriate for preschoolers:

- ❖ bear hugs
- ❖ firm back massages
- ❖ a sand pillow (see Chapter 6 for instructions) to sit on or lay in his lap during quiet periods
- ❖ roll the child in a heavy blanket or quilt during quiet periods

As you attempt to determine what is or is not effective with a child, remember that not every child who has SPD will benefit from all the recommendations listed here. Guidance from the child's therapist will help in selecting activities that are best suited to meet the sensory needs of the individual child. In all instances, maintain good communication with the parents as to what has been effective or ineffective for their child at preschool. This will assist the parents in finding appropriate home activities.

The next chapter provides more specific ways to meet the needs of individual children who have SPD, including suggestions for the preschool daily routine—morning circle, centers, outside play, mealtime, transitions, and rest time.

Practical Solutions to Meet the Needs of Individual Children During the Daily Routine

Designing the environment and implementing classroom strategies that meet the individual needs of young children are developmentally appropriate practices for preschool programs. Each part of the preschool daily routine, whether it is transitions, snack, or circle time, requires special considerations for children with Sensory Processing Disorder (SPD). The strategies that follow are designed to meet the needs of children with sensory processing issues, and they are practical and simple to carry out in any preschool environment. Many of these methods will benefit not only children with SPD, but also typically developing preschoolers.

Transitions

Young children often have difficulty with change in their environment. Therefore, transitions are sometimes disorganized and chaotic in preschool settings. One suggestion for meeting the needs of children with SPD is to use a consistent classroom schedule. A classroom routine helps the children learn when transitions will occur.

Prepare Ahead

Keep the preschoolers well informed of transitions. Presentation of the daily schedule works well in morning circle. Particularly at the beginning of the year, you may also want to review the daily schedule after lunch. Preschoolers thrive on routines and will quickly be able to tell you, "We go outside before lunch."

Always announce upcoming schedule changes several minutes before the transition. Young children are not aware of specific time frames, so do not tell them too far in advance. Maintain direct eye contact with children who have a very difficult time transitioning, and use simple phrases, such as, "In two minutes, we will go inside. Meet me at the fence."

Schedule changes will occur, so when you know in advance about a change, be sure to inform the children. You may want to design a signal or use a certain word to indicate to the preschoolers that a change is going to happen. For instance, during morning circle time, describe the "switcheroo" that will happen later in the day, "We have a switcheroo today. We will go to see a special program about fire safety after lunch. Then, we will come back to our room for center time."

There are many types of sensory-based cues that are effective for showing young children that a transition is going to happen. For instance, clap a rhythm to get the children's attention. Clapping your hands is a good auditory cue. Use specific patterns to identify certain types of transitions. Three short claps could signal that the children should begin cleaning up. Have children imitate the clapping pattern to assure that they are listening. If the children clap their hands, they will receive tactile and proprioceptive input, in addition to the auditory cue.

A visual cue for transitions is changing the lighting. Turn off the lights for several seconds; do not flicker the lights, because flashing lights can be overwhelming for young children. After you turn off the lights, use a quiet (rather than loud) voice to gain the children's attention. Firmly touching a child is a useful tactile cue for transitions—rub the child's arm or back firmly as you give verbal cues that it is time to change.

Many preschool teachers sing certain songs, such as "The Cleanup Song," to indicate upcoming transitions. You can also hum or whistle songs, such as "Whistle While You Work." Singing, humming, and whistling are effective in getting children to work toward a change in the classroom. Adding movement and heavy work activities to the music facilitates young children's alertness and participation in transitions. Try having the children march, stomp, or hop to the next activity.

Children who are Sensory Seekers or Sensory Under-Responders may be given special jobs to keep them on task during a transition. For example, the Sensory Seeker can open and close the door for the children to go in and out of the classroom, push a cart out to the playground, or carry a backpack full of books to the library. These are effective heavy work activities that keep children focused while providing sensory input in an appropriate way.

One suggestion for meeting the needs of children with SPD is to use a consistent classroom schedule. A classroom routine helps the children learn when transitions will occur.

Children who are Sensory Avoiders may not want to march or jump to the next activity. You can modify your approach to transitions by asking the child to count how many times another child hops along the way or identify colors or shapes that they spot. "Let's see how many circles you can find on the way to the playground."

Children who are Tactile Avoiders will sometimes come very slowly to line up or walk in a group. This is likely because they are fearful of the accidental touches they may receive when surrounded by children. Place the Tactile Avoider at the front of the line or the end of the line. Allow children to walk individually rather than in pairs. These changes can prevent negative outbursts and decrease the potential for bumping into a peer. Place children who are Proprioception Seekers (banging into objects and seeking heavy work) should be at the front of the line so they are less likely to push, hang on, or kick their peers.

Picture Schedule

A visual chart of the daily schedule provides a useful way to facilitate smooth transitions. Because daily schedules can change, the picture schedule (see Chapter 6 for instructions) should be designed as a flexible chart, so that pictures can be moved into a different order or other pictures may be substituted. To assist a child who has a particularly difficult time with transitions, visit the daily picture schedule before each transition. Another option is to create a personal picture schedule on a clipboard or in a small notebook for the child to keep in his cubby or carry with him for quick reference.

Circle Time

Children are usually asked to sit during circle time. Remember that most preschoolers can only attend for a short period for circle time activities. Typical activities include listening to a story, singing songs, discussing what they will be doing for the remainder of the day, and making center choices. Prepare children's bodies and brains for sitting by giving them enough movement before circle time. Schedule an active routine, such as center time or an outdoor/large motor activity before circle. Provide children with heavy work input that is calming while it incorporates movement. This may include telling the children to "creep like a cat" or "hop like a frog" to the circle. If children sit in chairs during circle time, have them pull or push their own chairs into the circle.

Maintaining Children's Attention

Preschoolers are kinesthetic learners who learn by moving their bodies within the environment. It is helpful to incorporate movement songs and poems into circle time. Music stimulates the brain and learning, especially in the areas of math, language, and motor skills. Ask the preschoolers to stand up and move along to songs, fingerplays, and poems. Vary the songs and movement games to keep the children engaged and interested.

In many preschool programs, children sit very close together in chairs or cross-legged on the floor, which does not allow much movement within the space. However, children need to move their bodies. To decrease the amount of times children get up, lie down, or roll around during circle time, seat them so that they can move gently within their personal space. Try using different surfaces for sitting on alternate days of the week to keep the environment stimulating. For instance, the children could sit on carpet squares on Monday, Wednesday, and Friday. Then, on Tuesday and Thursday, they could sit on small pillows. Other seating options include beanbag chairs, child-size rocking chairs, air pillows, or chairs with a cushion on top.

If a child is sensory seeking, he may roll around on the floor, run around the room, or touch his peers throughout circle time. Try placing a sand pillow (see Chapter 6 for instructions) in the preschooler's lap, or roll the

child in a heavy blanket. These methods give the child deep pressure, which is calming and helps the child maintain attention.

When you call on a preschooler who has SPD, give him extra time to respond. If there is a lot of sensory input coming in at the same time as the question, it may take more time to process the question. This may be the case when children are moving and talking to each other while you are pointing at a chart for the child to see. Maintain eye contact, and use simple, direct phrases, such as, "Is it hot or cold outside?" rather than, "What does the weather look like to you today, Joey? Is it hot or cold? Can you tell me?" After you ask the question and wait for several seconds, you may need to repeat the question to be sure that the child has heard and understood you.

Tactile Considerations

If the child is a Tactile Avoider, provide him with plenty of space to sit without touching another child. It may be helpful to place the child directly beside you. Accidental touches can also be prevented by sitting the child in a chair or on a particular spot on the floor. Use tape to draw a shape on the floor to give the child a clear boundary between him and the next child.

A child who is a Tactile Seeker may constantly touch other children, fiddle with his clothes, or chew on his shirt to get the sensory input he needs. A Tactile Under-Responder may not interact during circle activities. Add textures to circle time by allowing children to hold props, such as puppets or flannel pieces for the story board. Additionally, have the children sit on different textures of material, such as burlap, fur, or satin.

Children who cause distraction as they seek out sensory input may benefit from using a fidget toy like a small squishy ball, piece of textured fabric, or other little item. The child should be instructed to play with the fidget toy in his pocket or attach it to his belt loop. The child can fidget with the small object rather than touching other children. The fidget toy provides the child with the sensory input he seeks so he can focus on circle time activities.

Manipulatives/Fine Motor Activities

It is difficult for some preschoolers who have SPD to acquire fine motor skills, such as cutting with scissors, drawing, manipulating small objects with both hands, and handwriting. A developmentally appropriate preschool program includes time for young children to explore and participate in fine motor activities. Consider the type of materials used and design of the space. Facilitate important fine motor skills in young children by using the suggestions below.

Sensory-Smart Materials

Offer sensory-smart materials and tools during fine motor activities. Provide a variety of open-ended materials, such as paper, scissors, glue, tape, paint, puzzles, and games. In addition, offer an array of writing and drawing utensils, such as chubby crayons and pencils, standard crayons and pencils, markers, chalk, and paintbrushes. The child can select the writing tool that will allow him to be most successful.

A child needs a good awareness of his body's position to have adequate eye-hand coordination and strength for fine motor tasks. The objects listed below give deep pressure to the child's hands and arms and will promote greater body position sense. Young children who are Proprioceptive and/or Tactile Seekers and Under-Responders may benefit from using the following items:

- resistive materials, such as clay or playdough
- a battery-operated vibrating pen that wiggles and gives good input to the hand
- stiff paper, such as poster board, index cards, card stock, or sandpaper
- golf tees to push into Styrofoam
- a child's hammer and nails
- nuts and bolts to assemble
- good open-ended building materials that encourage the use of both hands, such as Legos and Lincoln Logs

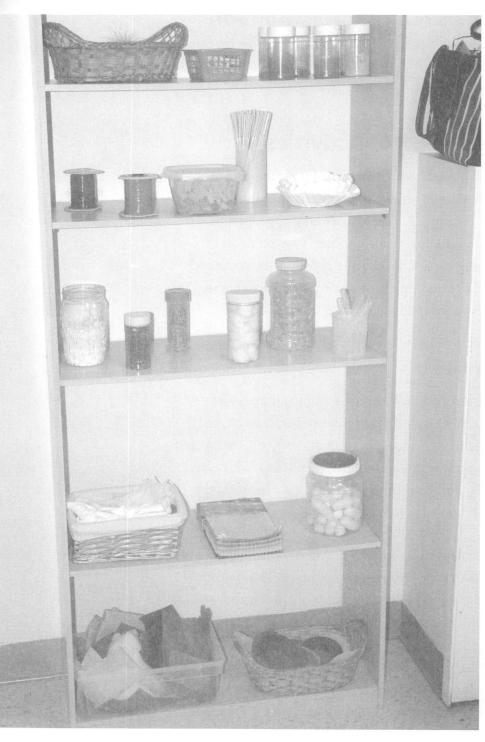

FUNctional Work Space

Consider how to present materials and tools. Is the work area cluttered? Are there too many choices of materials? Ensure that you organize all items in labeled containers that are safe and unbreakable. Store objects that are not in use, and give children easy access to the remaining objects to promote independence.

A clean work space is a must for children who are easily visually distracted. If the children work at tables, reduce the clutter on the tables by placing materials in under-the-table bins. Decrease glare on the tabletop by covering it with pastel-colored contact paper.

Consider where you place the child during fine motor activities. A child who is a Vestibular Seeker may need to stand or sit on a soft seat cushion so he can move around while working on his project. A child who is a Tactile Avoider may need to sit at the end of the table so another child does not accidentally knock or bump him. Children who are Proprioceptive (body position) Seekers or Under-Responders may do better lying on the floor or sitting in a beanbag chair.

Make sure that the child's feet are always planted firmly on the floor; it is very difficult for a child to write well or use good hand coordination if his feet are dangling from the chair. If the chair is the wrong size and not adjustable, place a phone book or other sturdy surface under the child's feet. If the child frequently falls out of his seat, you can place tennis balls over the feet of the chair. This will make it harder to knock the chair over, and the chair will be quieter as it moves across the floor.

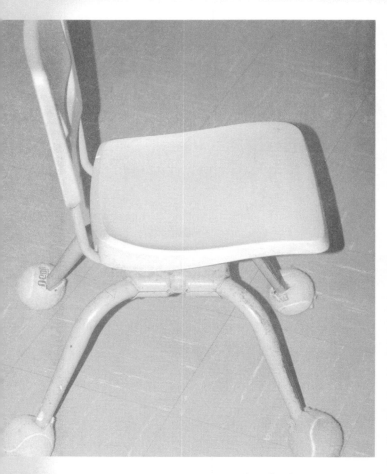

A child who is an Auditory Avoider may be over-stimulated by noises occurring in the room during fine motor play. For instance, the banging of hammers, screeching of chalk, and tearing of paper may be more auditory input than the child can tolerate. If the child cannot focus on an activity, allow him to wear earplugs or headphones with rhythmic, calming music.

Learning Centers

Learning centers work effectively in preschools because they actively engage young children in learning. Centers build on children's individual interests and capabilities. In centers, children can select or make guided choices of the materials they will use in centers. Offering different materials that provide a variety of sensory inputs in the centers supports the individual sensory needs of each preschooler.

Encouraging Movement Experiences

Children who are Vestibular Seekers or Proprioceptive Seekers need the opportunity to participate in motor activities inside the classroom. Children who are Vestibular Under-Responders or Proprioceptive Under-Responders will need encouragement to complete motor experiences. Large motor activities can be incorporated easily into centers, such as the Block Center, Gross Motor Center, and Music Center. In the Block Center, you can help children fill up baskets and trucks with wooden blocks. Then they can carry the baskets or push the trucks to the "new work site." In the Gross Motor Center, the children can bounce on a mini-trampoline or roll inside a carpet roll (see Chapter 6 for instructions). One child can sit in the middle of a blanket, while the other child pulls him around the space on a blanket ride. The Music Center encourages children to move, dance, or shake their bodies by offering diverse music choices. Include ribbon, scarves, shakers, drums, and maracas to facilitate different movement experiences.

Incorporating Proprioceptive and Tactile Input

The Art Center, Fine Motor Center, and Pre-Handwriting Center should provide opportunities for children to draw/write on vertical surfaces. Some examples of vertical surfaces include an easel, an incline board (see Chapter 6 for instructions), paper taped to the wall, or drawing on a chalk board/dry-erase board. Provide a Plexiglas painting wall (see Chapter 6 for instructions) for the children to use as a unique surface for creating art. Working on a vertical surface is a good method for adding proprioceptive input to the hands and upper body. These activities may also promote a good grasp of the writing tool.

In the Fine Motor Center and Art Center, young children can participate in other types of activities that will increase proprioceptive awareness. They can cut or tear thick paper, such as card stock, index cards, or construction paper. Young children can make and play with different types of clay and playdough. Painting with squeeze bottles or squirt bottles also adds proprioceptive input.

It is important to include materials with various textures so that children can choose the touch inputs they wish to receive. Offer watercolors, fingerpaint, glitter glue, and foam soap for painting in centers. The children can color or write on different textures of paper, such as sandpaper, foil, and wax paper. A blank piece of paper is less visually distracting for the child and encourages creative responses.

Facilitating Self-Awareness and Organization

Every preschool classroom should have a space where preschoolers can go to become calm and regain control. Young children also need to begin learning about an important life skill—self-awareness. A child must first learn to identify his feelings and sensory needs. Then he can begin to address his needs appropriately. A Private Place Center helps preschoolers develop a greater understanding of their emotions and how to manage their sensory processing needs. This center will be particularly useful for Sensory Avoiders who need a quiet place to go and get organized when they are over-stimulated.

The Private Place Center should remain available to young children throughout the year. It functions best in a low traffic area of the classroom. A large appliance box, tent, or an area with clear boundaries and only one entrance/exit works well. Fill it with pillows, blankets, a CD player with headphones, stuffed animals or comfort items, and several books. Do not include toys or objects that make noise.

The Private Place Center should not be used as a "time out" or punishment area for inappropriate behavior. If it is going to work well in the classroom, it must remain a safe place for children. When introducing the Private Place Center, include its purpose and rules for use. Examples of rules for this center include the following:

❖ Only one child at a time is allowed in the Private Place Center.
❖ You must tell a teacher before you enter the Private Place Center.
❖ You may use the Private Place Center when you are feeling _____ (sad, angry, or afraid).

Help individual children recognize when they need to enter the Private Place Center. For example, you might say, "Lelia, it looks like you are upset. I will help you go to the Private Place so you can calm down." Preschoolers may also need assistance in determining when to leave the center. It will take some children longer to get organized than others. Carefully monitor the child inside the center to see when he is ready to re-enter the classroom environment, "Lelia, I see that you are calm. Let's go back to the Home Living Center now." It will take time for children to learn how to use this center effectively. However, the Private Place Center has the potential for promoting social-emotional skills and appropriate management of the preschooler's own sensory processing skills.

Snack/Lunch

Mealtime should be a pleasurable experience in the preschool classroom. Unfortunately, many children with SPD are unable to relax and enjoy eating. Some children are over-stimulated by the variety of foods offered, the noises that surround them, or the child who accidentally bumps their elbow. Some are so sensitive to textures that they

are very picky eaters or do not eat at all. Other children are unable to feel the food in or around their mouths and are extremely messy eaters. The following sections include several simple solutions to help make meal and snack time more enjoyable for all preschoolers.

Sensory-Smart Foods

Begin by setting up the eating environment to be as calm and soothing as possible. Think about how relaxing a meal in a nice restaurant can be. Turn off some of the overhead lights and use table or floor lamps. Play soft classical music. Use quiet voices. Minimize the clutter on the table by having only necessary items, such as the children's plates, napkins, and silverware, on the table. These modifications will help decrease the chance that a child will be overloaded by too many sensory inputs before he even begins eating.

Consider the types of food you offer children. Try offering chewy food items to the preschoolers. Chewy foods provide "heavy work" sensory input through the mouth to help young children become more focused and attentive. A good calming activity is drinking a thick liquid through a straw. Make smoothies, frozen drinks, or milkshakes for the children to sample. Chewy foods are also good choices for a child who overstuffs his mouth for proprioception input. Fruit chews, dried fruit, beef jerky, raisins, bread, and cheese sticks are other foods to help children focus.

If the children are inattentive or overly drowsy, provide crunchy foods, such as crackers, pretzels, and raw vegetables to help the child be alert. Crunchy foods are a nice choice for afternoon snack, to wake up preschoolers. Do not provide foods with high sugar content that give children a quick burst of energy and then leave them feeling lethargic.

A good calming activity is drinking a thick liquid through a straw.

Toileting

Sometimes, going into a bathroom can be overwhelming for young children. There are many noises, smells, and sights that preschoolers may find frightening or discomforting. Changes can be made in the environment to promote independence in the bathroom.

It is particularly important that the toilets be child-size. If they are not, place a stool or block on the floor under the seat for the children to use as a step stool and to place their feet on when sitting. The stool gives them greater balance on the toilet and helps in preventing the child from feeling as though he is going to fall off or into the toilet.

With a lot of sensory input, preschoolers may feel lost and unsure as to what to do in the bathroom, and in what order. Place a visual chart with pictures of the hand washing sequence beside the sink to help preschoolers follow the appropriate steps of hand washing.

If the child fears the sound of running water, pre-fill the sink with warm, soapy water for him to wash his hands or use no-rinse hand sanitizer. If the sound of the toilet flushing is over-stimulating, the child could wear earplugs or headphones with white noise or calming music while in the bathroom. Another way to decrease auditory and visual inputs is to allow the child to enter the bathroom without peers. To reduce echoes, encourage preschoolers to use quiet voices inside the bathroom.

Rest

To design a restful environment, it is important to consider the children's sensory needs. A well-rested child is more likely to participate in preschool activities later in the day. A child who has had some rest has a greater tolerance for sensory inputs and is less likely to become overwhelmed by the environment. The following suggestions will help get the children organized, calm, and ready for a rest.

Calming Environment

A peaceful and soothing environment is key to a successful rest time. The first step in this process is darkening the room, which may be carried out by turning off lights, dimming lights, and closing shades or blinds. Flashing lights stimulate; if light flickers through the window or blinds, use a curtain or sheet to cover it completely.

Preschool programs often play music to drown out extraneous noise. However, some types of music and the volume level may be overwhelming for children. When playing music, keep the volume low and select rhythmic, soothing music that does not change tempos frequently. Another option is to use a white noise machine during rest time.

Many children sleep in a cluttered environment full of visual stimulation. Instead of resting, they may look at their surroundings or play with the objects they see. Provide children with an environment with little or no clutter and clear boundaries, which may include placing a child in a corner or next to a wall or bookcase. Remove toys and objects at eye level and place a sheet over shelves or bookcases to decrease visual distraction.

Promote independence and help the children feel a sense of control by letting them set up their own rest areas. Carrying a mat or cot to their rest area is a good calming activity. Children can also put the sheet on top of the mat themselves and carry their blankets and comfort items to the mat. In this way, they actively participate in preparing their special place for rest.

Simple Rest-Time Modifications

Once the room has been turned into a peaceful haven, consider the individual needs of the preschool children. Children who are Tactile Seekers, Proprioception Seekers, Tactile Under-Responders, or Proprioception Under-Responders may benefit from being rolled up in a heavy blanket. Offer a firm backrub to the child to help him calm down. Firm, rhythmic patting on the back may also help a child settle down for a rest. Tactile Avoiders may need their mats placed far away from other children, so they do not stay awake fearing that another child may accidentally bump or roll into them. A child who is an Auditory Avoider may need to wear earplugs to decrease awareness of noises from other children or other environmental noise makers, such as the heating and air conditioning unit.

Playground or Gym

It is appropriate for preschoolers to learn important large motor skills, such as running, jumping, and climbing. The playground and gymnasium provide excellent open spaces that encourage these motor skills. Large motor activities require a very small amount of equipment. Open-ended equipment will keep children interested for a long time. When you see that the children are no longer playing with certain toys, remove them for a while and reintroduce them later.

Sensory-Smart Equipment for the Playground or Gym

* soft balls of all sizes
* plastic containers or trash cans for collection and storage of equipment, and to throw balls into or push around
* tire swing (outside) (see Chapter 6 for instructions) or Sit 'n Spin (inside)
* riding toys
* climbing structure or rope ladder
* wagon
* hula hoops
* sandbox (outside) or ball pit (inside)

Remember that one of the best ways to get a child involved is for you to be actively involved. Model appropriate interactions and large motor experiences to the preschoolers by joining in the fun!

Heavy Work/Play

Incorporate heavy work activities in outside or gym playtime. This includes catching and throwing heavy balls, running, hopping, and skipping. Climbing is a heavy work activity that also builds strength and coordination. A great organizing activity is to allow a child to pull one or two children in a wagon. This gives proprioceptive input to the child pulling the wagon and vestibular input to the child riding in the wagon. A crash pad (see Chapter 6 for instructions) can be used inside for children to jump into, on top of, and roll around on. The crash pad provides a soft, safe landing choice for children seeking more proprioceptive input.

Keep Your Feet on the Ground, Please!

Many children who are Vestibular Avoiders are afraid to have their feet off the ground. Facilitate large motor activities where children keep their feet on the ground, such as parachute games or animal walks. Blowing bubbles is a good outdoor activity because it promotes calmness and attention. Plus, it is a lot of fun! Children can try to catch the bubbles and pop them with their hands. Another activity is to build an obstacle course using three or four areas. For instance, jump into hula hoops, crawl through a tunnel, and walk down the line. Begin by demonstrating how to navigate the obstacle course; you may need to guide the child through it the first time. Or, allow the child to stand back and watch the other children as you describe the steps in the course.

Let the Child Be Your Guide

Observe and listen to the child. For Vestibular Avoiders, ask yourself the question: "Is he afraid of certain movements or types of equipment?" Trust his feelings and let him show what he needs. Do not force him to play on the playground equipment. Think about ways of modifying the environment to promote involvement in movement experiences. Start with simple activities. If the child will not get on the swing, consider lowering it so that his feet can touch the ground. Just sitting in the swing is a big first step. Praise the child for attempting to participate, by saying, "Josh, I really like the way you are sitting on the swing."

What Have You Learned?

You have expanded your understanding of sensory integration (SI), which may assist you in identifying children in your classroom who may have SPD. You have gained information about the different types of sensory processing problems, which includes Sensory Avoiders, Sensory Seekers, and Sensory Under-Responders in the areas of visual, auditory, tactile, vestibular, and proprioceptive sensations. Now it is time to use your awareness of sensory processing to make simple changes in your environment and the daily classroom routine. These modifications can have a great effect on young children's learning.

Building and Creating Low-Cost Items

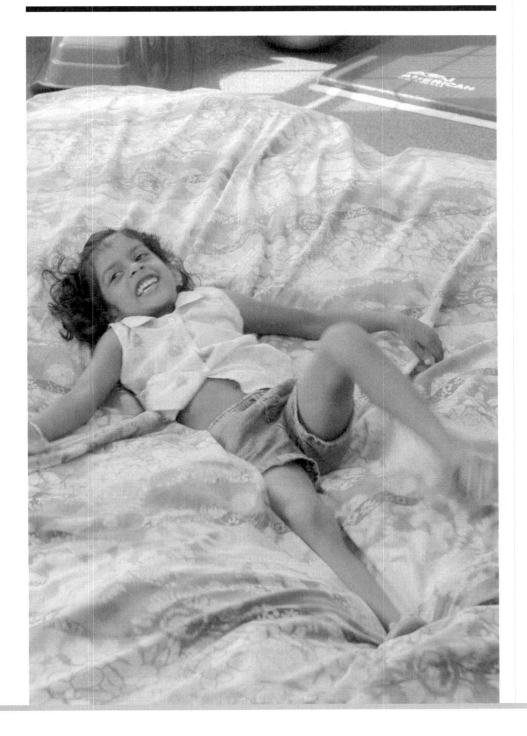

There are many simple-to-make items that will provide increased opportunities for young children in your classroom to use their developing sensory abilities. These materials are low cost and the items provide great benefits for your children.

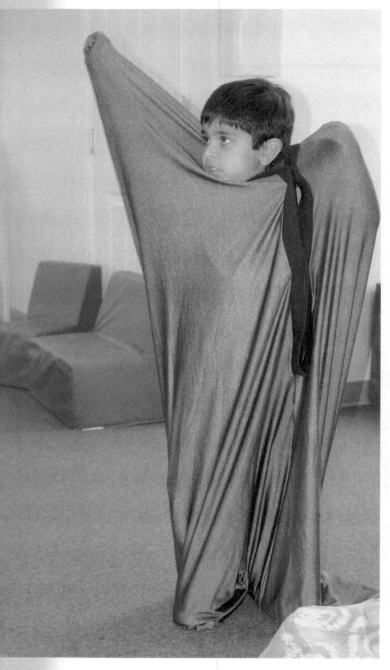

Body Sock

The body sock is a fun piece of indoor equipment that promotes proprioception (body position) and provides tactile input to preschoolers. This item was inspired by Kimberly Dye's Body Sox™. Preschoolers can climb completely inside the sock or leave their heads outside. Children can see through the material when it is stretched. As preschoolers move inside the body sock, they develop balance, coordination, and motor skills, such as walking, running, rolling, and hopping. The remaining strips of Lycra make fantastic scarves for dress up.

Materials

1 ⅛ yards of Lycra material (at least 56" wide)
24" of hook Velcro
24" of loop Velcro
thread and needle or sewing machine

Procedure

1. Cut Lycra material to 41" x 56".
2. Fold in half (41" x 28") and sew the side and bottom of Lycra material together. Fasten the top edge of the tube, leaving a 24" opening in the middle for Velcro closure.
3. Sew hook Velcro on one side of the top opening and loop Velcro on the other side of the top opening. This provides a way for the preschooler to climb inside the body sock and close it up.

Carpet Roll

Children can use a carpet roll to climb inside, around, and over. The carpet roll may be used in the classroom to encourage large motor skills and provide vestibular (movement and balance) input. Young children can roll inside the carpet roll to give them an even greater movement sensation. Visit a local carpet dealer and ask for the carpet roll that remains when the carpet is sold. The carpet dealer may even donate carpet remnants to cover the roll. A 4' carpet roll is an ample size and may be cut to fit your space.

Materials

cardboard roll from inside roll of carpet

Note: The cylinder must be large enough and sturdy enough for a young child to climb inside.

utility knife or electric knife (adult use only)

durable carpet or vinyl to cover the cylinder (carpeting will cushion the cylinder, while vinyl protects and supports the surface for long-term use)

glue

heavy-duty staples and stapler (adult use only)

duct tape

Procedure

1. Cut the cardboard roll using the utility knife or an electric knife, to make it 4' long (or a length that will fit the space).
2. Cover the roll with durable, washable carpet.
3. Staple carpet to the roll and cover the staples with duct tape.
4. Glue durable, washable carpet or material to the inside of the roll. Gluing fabric to the outside of the roll (over the carpet) is optional, and it may make the roll more durable.

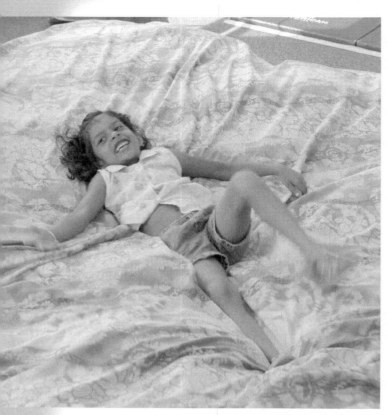

Crash Pad

The crash pad acts as a safe indoor spot for preschoolers to receive proprioceptive (body position) input. Young children can gain a greater awareness of their bodies by jumping, rolling, and crashing into this big, soft pillow.

Materials

2 full- or queen-size flat sheets (size selected will be determined by the size of the space available)

2 twin- or full-size flat sheets (one size smaller than the first two sheets)

scrap foam or pillows

thread and needle or sewing machine

Procedure

1. Sew the edges of the smaller pair of sheets together, leaving a large opening on one end.
2. Stuff the sack with large pieces of scrap foam or pillows, filling the sack as full as possible, as some settling will occur.
3. Sew the opening of the crash pad closed.
4. Sew three sides of the larger pair of sheets together, leaving one end completely open, to make a washable cover for the crash pad.
5. Stuff the crash pad inside the cover, which may be removed and washed as needed.

Incline Board

An incline board provides a stable and elevated surface on which preschoolers can draw, paint, or write. The elevated surface provides extra resistance to drawing experiences, which increases body position (proprioception) input. An incline of 20° will help a child use an appropriate grasp of the utensil. The incline board may be used on a tabletop or on the floor.

Materials

tri-wall (3-ply) or heavy-duty cardboard (at least 14½" x 19")
Note: Tri-wall cardboard may be collected as scraps from a packaging company.
utility knife or electric knife for cutting cardboard (adult use only)
hot-glue gun and hot glue (adult use only)
solid-color contact paper

Procedure

1. Cut cardboard into the following four pieces (as shown in the diagram):
    ❖ 1 piece measuring 15" x 14"
    ❖ 2 triangle-shape pieces with a length of 14" and a height of 4" at the tallest point
    ❖ 1 piece 15" x ½"
2. Hot glue the pieces of cardboard to form an incline board.
3. Glue the ½" strip to the bottom of the board to keep paper from sliding.
4. Cover incline with solid-color contact paper for greater durability.

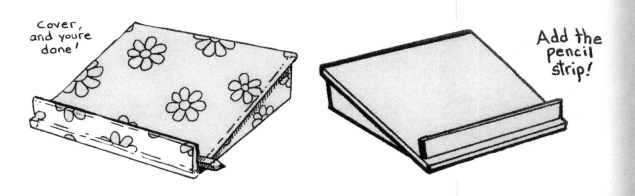

Cover, and you're done!

Add the pencil strip!

Picture Schedule

A picture schedule is a useful tool to assist preschoolers with transitions. Morning circle is an appropriate time to use a picture schedule to help prepare the young children for their daily activities. Providing preschoolers with information about how the day will flow helps them to transition more smoothly. The picture schedule is also an appropriate visual input for preschoolers who are Visual Seekers.

Materials

camera
laminating materials or clear contact paper
sticky-back hook-and-loop Velcro or magnetized tape
poster board
large envelope or folder

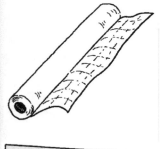

Procedure

1. Take pictures of activities that occur on a regular basis in the classroom, such as circle time, free choice, center time, lunch, bathroom, rest time, and so on. Also take pictures of activities that occasionally need to be substituted into the schedule, such as a field trip or special visitor.
2. Label each picture and attach individual pictures to poster board or laminate the pictures so they are stiff and durable.
3. Place sticky-back Velcro to the back of each picture and to a large piece of poster board. Alternately, magnetized tape may be used.
4. Attach an envelope or folder to the poster board to hold extra pictures.

Attach to board and cover with contact paper.

Plexiglas Painting Wall

Preschoolers who are Tactile Seekers and Tactile Under-Responders need opportunities to draw and paint on vertical surfaces. Upright work surfaces are useful to increase proprioception (body position) input and may also promote good grasp of utensils. A Plexiglas painting wall provides children with a vertical surface to develop their creations. Fingerpainting on the Plexiglas painting wall is a great tactile experience for preschoolers and is easy to clean up.

Materials

⅛" clear Plexiglas (cut to size of your wall space)
4–8 screws or clips
screwdriver
Plastic tarp or shower curtain

Procedure

1. Screw Plexiglas into the wall at preschoolers' eye level.
2. Cover the floor with plastic or a shower curtain.

Sand Pillow

Deep pressure input is calming and helps children focus. Sand pillows provide deep pressure to young children, as they sit with them in their laps. These are especially useful for quiet periods, such as circle time. Sand pillows also encourage body position awareness. Sand pillows should be used for no more than 15 minutes every two hours. A sand pillow should weigh approximately 10% of the child's body weight. To simplify, make a three-pound pillow for three-year-olds and a four-pound pillow for four- and five-year-olds.

Materials

2 pillowcases
3 lbs. of white sand for three-year-olds;
    4 lbs. of white sand for four- or five-year-olds, or aquarium gravel
thread and needle or sewing machine

Procedure

1. Place the sand inside one pillowcase.
2. Sew the open end of the pillowcase tightly closed so that sand cannot leak out.
3. Use the other pillowcase to cover the sand pillow, so it can be removed and washed easily.

Sound Panel

Children who are Auditory Avoiders may be over-stimulated by loud noises. Inexpensive and easily constructed panels can provide sound absorption in the classroom. Place sound panels on the wall to reduce the sound level in a noisy area or the entire room.

Materials

1 sheet of 4' x 8' sound board 1" thick (available at home improvement stores)
handsaw (adult use only)
loosely woven burlap or other fabric
heavy-duty stapler (adult use only)
duct tape

Procedure

1. Cut the sound panel into two 4' x 4' pieces.
2. Cover each piece of the board with fabric on one side.
3. Staple the fabric to the back of the board.
4. Cover staples and fabric edges with duct tape.
5. Attach to the wall in selected location to assist with noise reduction.

Tire Swing

A tire swing is a wonderful piece of outdoor playground equipment. When a tire swing is hung horizontally, more than one child can swing on it, which promotes social interaction between preschoolers. Children receive vestibular (movement and balance) input while swinging on a tire swing. Visit a local tire center to request the donation of a large car, truck, or tractor tire. A tire that is defective or irregular works well, and old tires can be spray-painted with nontoxic exterior enamel paint. After you hang the swing, use a heavy duty drill to make holes in the underside of the tire for water to drain from the swing.

Materials

a car, truck, or tractor tire

Safety Note: Do not use steel-belted tires, as they contain steel wires that can come through the surface and cause injury.

nylon rope or ¼" cable for suspension

heavy-duty swivel

The following are needed for each suspension point:
     2½" fender washer
     2½" machine bolt
     2 1½" steel washers

Procedure

For more specific information on constructing a tire swing, see Frost's (1992) book, *Play and Playscapes*.

1. Select a tire that will hold 2–3 children.
2. Drill holes in the tire that will be turned horizontally.
3. Suspend rope or cable from three positions on the top of the tire.
4. Attach the three pieces of rope/cable to the swivel.
5. Hang from swing set or tree.
6. Other uses for old tires include tunnels, bridges, walls, and rafts.

References

Ayres, A. J. 1973. *Sensory integration and learning disorders.* Los Angeles: Western Psychological Services.

Bundy, A., S. J. Lane, & E. A. Murray, eds. 2002. *Sensory integration: Theory and practice (2nd ed.).* Philadelphia: F.A. Davis.

Frost, J. L. 1992. *Play and playscapes.* Clifton Park, NY: Thomson Delmar Learning.

Kranowitz, C. S. 2005. *Preschool SENSE (SENsory Scan for Educators): A collaborative tool for occupational therapists and early childhood teachers.* Las Vegas: Sensory Resources.

Kranowitz, C. S. 2006. *The out-of-sync child: Recognizing and coping with sensory processing disorder, Revised Edition.* New York: Penguin Group.

Miller, L. J., S. A. Cermak, S. J. Lane, M. E. Anzalone, & J. A. Koomar. Summer 2004. Position statement on terminology related to Sensory integration dysfunction. *S.I. Focus* magazine.

Miller, L. J., & D.A. Fuller, 2006. *Sensational kids: Hope and help for children with sensory processing disorder (SPD).* New York: Penguin Group.

Roley, S. S., E. I. Blanche, & R. C. Schaaf, eds. 2001. *Understanding the Nature of Sensory Integration with Diverse Populations.* San Antonio, TX: Therapy Skill Builders.

Wilbarger, P. & Wilbarger, J. L. 1991. *Sensory Defensiveness in Children Aged 2-12: An Intervention Guide for Parents and Other Caretakers.* Van Nuys, CA: Avanti Educational Programs.

Resources

Ayres, A. J. 2005. *Sensory integration and the child: 25th anniversary edition (14th ed.).* Los Angeles: Western Psychological Services.

Bissel, J., J. Fisher, C. Owens, & P. Polcyn. 1998. *Sensory motor handbook: a guide for implementing and modifying activities in the classroom.* San Antonio: Therapy Skill Builders, 1998.

Dejean, V. & Freer, A. 2002. What is sensory integration? Hand-out from Spectrum Center, Inc., (301) 657-0988 or www.spectrumcenter.com.

Dunn, W. 1999. *Sensory profile: User's manual.* San Antonio: Psychological Corporation.

Grooms, J. 2001. *The scoop on sensory integration: A resource created for teachers and paraprofessionals.* (16-page booklet.) available from Pocket Full of Therapy.

Henry, D. 1998. *Tool chest for teachers, parents & students: A handbook to facilitate self regulation.* Youngtown, AZ: Henry OT Services.

Isbell, C., & R.T. Isbell. 2005. *The inclusive learning center book for preschool children with special needs.* Beltsville, MD: Gryphon House.

Isbell, R., & B. Exelby. 2001. *Early learning environments that work.* Beltsville, MD: Gryphon House.

Koomar, J. A., Friedman, B., & Woolf, illus. 1998. *The hidden senses: Your muscle sense and the hidden senses: Your balance sense.* Hugo, MN: PDP Press.

Koomar, J., C.S. Kranowitz, D.I. Sava, E. Haber, L. Balzer-Martin, & S. Szklut. 2004. *Answers to questions teachers ask about sensory integration (2nd ed.).* Las Vegas: Sensory Resources.

Kranowitz, C. S. 2006. *The out-of-sync child has fun, revised edition: Activities for kids with sensory processing disorder.* New York: Penguin Group.

Schneider, C.C. 2001. *Sensory secrets: How to jump-start learning in Children.* Concerned Communications: Siloam Springs, Arkansas

S. I. Focus Magazine. www.SIFocus.com.

Williams, M.S. & S. Shellenberger, 1992). *An Introduction to "How Does Your Engine Run?" The Alert Program for Self-Regulation.* Albuquerque: Therapy Works.

Glossary

Attention Deficit Hyperactivity Disorder (ADHD) – A condition usually seen in children that is characterized by inattention, hyperactivity, and impulsiveness.

Auditory Avoider – See Sensory Avoider.

auditory defensiveness – Another term for Auditory Avoider – see Sensory Avoider.

Auditory Seeker – See Sensory Seeker.

auditory sense – The sensory system that is responsible for identifying sounds, understanding what has been heard, and preparing for a response.

Auditory Under-Responder – See Sensory Under-Responder.

child clinical psychologist (Ph.D.) – Adolescent and child clinical psychologists conduct scientific research and provide psychological services to infants, toddlers, children, and adolescents. The research and practices of clinical child psychology are focused on understanding, preventing, diagnosing, and treating psychological, cognitive, emotional, developmental, behavioral, and family problems of children.

Child Find Program – A publicly funded program under IDEA intended to identify, locate, and evaluate/assess infants and toddlers with potential developmental delays or disabilities. The program may have different names in different communities (for example, community screening) and may include public education about child development and parenting.

child psychiatrist (M.D.) – A medical doctor who has completed two to three years of an adult psychiatric residency and two additional years of a child psychiatry fellowship.

choice board – This is a visual representation of the possible choices in Center time and a place where a child can display his or her Center selection.

clip lights – A lamp that has a metal neck with a clip on the base. It adjusts so children are able to focus the light right where it is needed most.

deep pressure – A firm tactile stimulus that causes receptors in the skin to respond (Example: hug or pat). Another term for firm touch.

developmental pediatrician – A pediatrician with specialized training in children's social, emotional, and intellectual development as well as their health and physical growth.

developmentally appropriate – Activities and educational experiences that match the child's age and stage of development.

dimmer switch – An electrical device that allows for adjustment of light levels from nearly dark to full light by simply turning a knob or sliding a lever.

family practice physician – A physician who deals with the prevention, diagnosis, and treatment of illnesses in all members of the family.

fidget toy – A small object or toy for a child to manipulate in his hands so as to decrease whole body movements. A fidget toy may assist the child in maintaining attention.

fine motor – Movement of the small muscles in the fingers (for example, stringing beads, drawing, writing, or cutting with scissors). Another term for small motor.

firm touch – See deep pressure.

full spectrum lighting – Electric light sources that simulate the visible and ultraviolet (UV) spectrum of natural light.

gross motor – Movement of the large muscles in the arms, legs, and back (for example, walking, running, and jumping). Another term for large motor.

heavy work – activities that are strenuous to complete (for example, carrying a heavy backpack or pulling a wagon loaded with building blocks).

hypersensitive – Over-sensitive to sensory input.

hyposensitive – Under-sensitive to sensory input.

Individuals with Disabilities Education Act (IDEA) – A United States federal law, most recently amended in 2004, which is meant to ensure "a free appropriate public education" for students with disabilities, designed to their individualized needs in the least restrictive environment. The act requires that public schools provide necessary learning aids, testing modifications, and other educational accommodations to children with disabilities. The act also establishes due process in providing accommodations. Children, whose learning is hampered by disabilities not interfering with his/her ability to function in a general classroom, may qualify for similar accommodations under section 504 of the Rehabilitation Act of 1973 or the Americans with Disabilities Act (ADA).

kinesthetic – Use of the body to gain control and learn about physical capabilities, develop body awareness, and gain understanding of the world. It is another way of knowing and feeling.

large motor – See gross motor.

light touch – A soft or mild tactile stimulus that causes receptors in the skin to respond (for example, a kiss).

occupational therapist (OT) – See pediatric occupational therapist.

open-ended – An activity that allows for many different responses to a problem; divergent thinking is needed.

organize – To assume a state of mental competence, so as to be ready to perform a task.

pediatric occupational therapist (OT) – A health care professional who helps children overcome physical or social problems due to illness or disability. OTs are skilled in adapting children's environment so that they can participate in the occupations of childhood: play, school, and self-care.

pediatrician (M.D.) – A medical doctor with specialized training in caring for the physical health, growth, and development of children.

personal space – The sense of invisible boundaries surrounding an individual's body and separating one from others, the encroachment of which may cause anxiety.

picture schedule – A series of pictures that demonstrate what is supposed to occur within an area or timeframe.

Proprioception Avoider – See Sensory Avoider.

Proprioception Seeker – See Sensory Seeker.

Proprioception Under-Responder – See Sensory Under-Responder.

proprioceptive (body awareness) sense – The unconscious awareness of sensations coming from the muscles and joints, which provides information about where each part of the body is and how it is moving. Another term for proprioception.

Sensory Avoider – The child is over-sensitive to certain sensory inputs: visual, auditory, tactile, vestibular (movement and balance), and/or proprioception (body position). The child demonstrates behaviors that help him avoid experiencing these sensations.

sensory diet – A planned activity program that an OT designs to meet the sensory needs of an individual child with a Sensory Processing Disorder (SPD).

Sensory Discrimination Disorder (SDD) – Experiencing difficulty in telling the difference between and among sensory stimulation.

sensory integration (SI) – The brain's process of taking in and effectively responding to information from all sensory inputs: vision, hearing (auditory), touch (tactile), taste (gustatory), smell (olfactory), movement (vestibular), and body awareness (proprioception).

Sensory Integration Dysfunction (SI Dysfunction) – Another term for Sensory Processing Disorder (SPD).

Sensory Integration Theory – A concept explaining the relationship between the brain and behavior.

Sensory Modulation Disorder (SMD) – An inability to sort out and control appropriate strength and type of response to sensory input.

sensory processing – See sensory integration.

Sensory Processing Disorder (SPD) – Problems in the way the brain takes in and responds to information from all sensory inputs: visual, auditory, tactile, vestibular (movement and balance), proprioception (body position), gustatory (taste), and/or olfactory (smell), so that the child is unable to interact effectively in everyday life.

Sensory Seeker – The child is under-sensitive to certain sensory inputs: visual, auditory, tactile, vestibular (movement and balance), and/or proprioception (body position). The child seems to crave or seek out these types of sensation.

Sensory Under-Responder – The child does not respond enough to certain sensory inputs (visual, auditory, tactile, vestibular, and/or proprioception) or does not react as quickly as necessary to those sensory inputs. The child may need sensory inputs that are stronger or last longer before he or she will respond.

Sensory-Based Motor Disorder (SBMD) – A problem with movement that is due to inefficient sensory processing.

sensory-smart – Activities that provide appropriate sensory inputs.

small motor – See fine motor.

Tactile Avoider – See Sensory Seeker. Another term for tactile defensiveness.

Tactile Under-Responder – See Sensory Under-Responder.

tactile defensiveness – The tendency to respond to unexpected, light touch sensations in a negative or emotional manner.

Tactile Seeker – See Sensory Seeker.

tactile sense – The sensory system responsible for identifying touch input, understanding what has been felt, and preparing for a response.

vestibular (movement and balance) sense – The sensory system responding to the pull of gravity and providing information about the head's position in relation to the earth's surface. This sense coordinates movement of the eyes, head, and body, which impacts balance, vision, hearing, and emotional security.

Vestibular Avoider – See Sensory Avoider.

Vestibular Seeker – See Sensory Seeker.

Vestibular Under-Responder – See Sensory Under-Responder.

Visual Avoider – See Sensory Avoider.

Visual Seeker – See Sensory Seeker.

visual sense – The sensory system responsible for identifying sight input, understanding what has been seen, and preparing for a response.

Visual Under-Responder – See Sensory Under-Responder.

white noise machine – A device that produces random sound, which is somewhat like air escaping from a balloon. Often used to protect privacy by masking distant conversations, they are also sold as sleep aids. Such machines often can produce other soothing sounds such as rain, wind, and ocean waves.

Appendix

Visual Avoider: Red Flags

The Visual Avoider may

* avoid sunlight and other bright light (for example, the child may want to wear sunglasses or hat inside and outside);
* refuse to participate in activities where there are too many children involved (because the children are moving around and stimulating the visual system);
* get motion sickness from too much visual input;
* avoid eye contact with adults or peers;
* be unable to determine distances (for example, the child may bump into a bookcase or room divider);
* have headaches or nausea when he or she has overused his or her eyes;
* close his or her eyes or try to avoid balls or other objects thrown to him or her; or
* rub his or her eyes.

Visual Seeker: Red Flags

The Visual Seeker may

* stare at bright lights, flickering lights, or direct sunlight;
* stare at his or her fingers as he or she moves them or at objects moving in space (for example, ceiling fans, flags, or mobiles);
* move around or shake his or her head during drawing or fine motor activities; or
* hold objects close to his or her face to look at them.

Visual Under-Responder: Red Flags

The Visual Under-Responder may

* be unaware of new objects, materials or people in the environment;
* stare at bright lights or moving objects with a faraway look in his or her eyes;
* fall over or bump into new obstacles inside or outside; or
* have difficulty catching balls or getting out of the way of moving objects or people because he or she responds too slowly.

Note: If you suspect a child may have SPD in the visual area, the child should have a thorough vision screening with an optometrist to rule out basic vision problems.

The publisher grants permission for this page to be photocopied for distribution for teacher's classroom use only.
© Gryphon House, Inc. 800.638.0928. www.ghbooks.com

Auditory Avoider: Red Flags

The Auditory Avoider may

❖ demonstrate excessive emotions (for example, crying, screaming, anger) when he or she hears a sudden noise such as an alarm, thunder, siren, or horn;

❖ demonstrate excessive emotions when the noise level in the room increases (for example, during center time);

❖ put his or her fingers in his or her ears and yell or hum, to drown out certain sounds (for example, a train);

❖ be upset by common noises such as a toilet flushing, water running, or background music; or

❖ demonstrate excessive emotions when he or she hears high-pitched sounds such as a drill, whistle, chalk squeaking, or metal clinking.

Auditory Seeker: Red Flags

The Auditory Seeker may

❖ turn the volume of music up very loud;

❖ talk very loudly inside the classroom;

❖ hold musical toys or other toys that make noise directly to his or her ear to listen;

❖ make noisy sounds such as clapping, yelling, banging objects, or singing loudly;

❖ enjoy high-pitched noises (such as a drill, a whistle, or bells); or

❖ crave common noises such as that of a toilet flushing, water running, or the air conditioner humming.

Auditory Under-Responder: Red Flags

The Auditory Under-Responder may

❖ seem unaware of typical sounds in the classroom or outside;

❖ respond slowly or not at all to verbal requests; or

❖ pay attention only to extremely loud noises or music that is boisterous or has an unusual rhythm.

Note: If you suspect a child may be an Auditory Seeker, the child should have a thorough auditory screening to rule out basic hearing problems.

The publisher grants permission for this page to be photocopied for distribution for teacher's classroom use only.
© Gryphon House, Inc. 800.638.0928. www.ghbooks.com

Tactile Avoider: Red Flags

The Tactile Avoider may

* respond to light or unexpected touch in a negative manner (for example, hitting, biting) or with excessive emotions (for example, crying, screaming);
* avoid messy activities in the classroom (for example, painting, gluing);
* run away or hide when a tactile experience is introduced;
* not like to be kissed or touched, but may initiate hugs or firm touch;
* walk at the front or end of the line to avoid being touched;
* be a picky eater;
* be very clean and wash his or her hands immediately after any activity;
* appear stubborn or inflexible;
* be excessively ticklish;
* dislike going barefoot;
* react with extreme emotion or anger when face is washed;
* refuse to hold hands with someone else;
* overreact to minor bumps, cuts, or scrapes;
* complain about certain types of clothing or tags in shirts;
* require that his or her shoes be tied extra tight, or complain about socks being bunched or twisted;
* try to talk his or her way out of touching or playing with textures: "My mommy told me not to get dirty;"
* have difficulty establishing friendships in the classroom, because he or she stays away from other children to avoid getting touched unexpectedly or lightly;
* walk on tiptoes; or
* refuse to wear hats or dress-up clothes.

Tactile Seeker: Red Flags

The Tactile Seeker may

* appear to crave touch (for example, the child will fingerpaint for a long time);
* constantly put objects in his or her mouth;
* love messy experiences;
* bump into things or people;
* be unable to keep his or her hands to him- or herself;
* stuff his or her mouth with food;
* rub textures over his or her arms or legs;
* prefer spicy, hot, or very cold foods;
* get very close to others when playing or talking;
* rub or bite his or her own skin; or
* touch others constantly.

Tactile Under-Responder: Red Flags

The Tactile Under-Responder may

* seem unaware of a messy or dirty face or body;
* not respond to gentle touches;
* lack interest in creative arts (for example, paint, glue, clay);
* have difficulty manipulating small toys or objects;
* not seem to notice cold or hot temperature;
* seem unaware of different textures (for example, hard, scratchy, soft);
* not notice that clothing is wet or dirty;
* be slow with potty-training; or
* be slow to learn how to undress/dress self.

Note: If you suspect a child may have SPD in the tactile area, the child should have a thorough vision screening with an optometrist to rule out basic vision problems.

The publisher grants permission for this page to be photocopied for distribution for teacher's classroom use only.
© Gryphon House, Inc. 800.638.0928. www.ghbooks.com

Vestibular Avoider: Red Flags

The Vestibular Avoider may

* be timid and cautious with movement experiences (a non-risk taker);
* be fearful of playground equipment such as slides, swings, jungle gyms, or monkey bars;
* get carsick, even on short trips;
* have poor self-esteem, because he or she will not play with others, particularly outside;
* be afraid of elevators or escalators;
* be fearful of heights or dislike when his or her feet are off the ground;
* be afraid to climb or descend stairs (for example, hold the railing with both hands);
* appear stubborn or uncooperative;
* be unable to ride a tricycle, bicycle, or other age-appropriate riding toys;
* appear manipulative, especially in cases where he or she feels a lack of control (For example, the child may say, "Let's go play under the tree. Only babies go on the slide."); or
* be clumsy or uncoordinated.

Vestibular Seeker: Red Flags

The Vestibular Seeker may

* take safety risks inside and outside;
* not be able to sit still;
* be impulsive (do things before thinking);
* run instead of walk;
* be in constant motion (for example, wiggle, fidget, rock back and forth, bounce on his or her bottom);
* push every movement experience to the extreme (for example, attempt to swing over the top of the swing set);
* not get dizzy, no matter how much he or she has been spinning around; or
* enjoy movement experiences more than other children.

Vestibular Under-Responder: Red Flags

The Vestibular Under-Responder may

* appear accident prone (for example, falls or trips and does not catch him- or herself);
* be less coordinated than other preschoolers;
* not notice movements or changes in movement (for example, pushing high on a swing);
* not like new movement experiences;
* tend to sit, stand, or lay around more than other preschoolers; or
* appear easily tired or lazy.

Note: If you suspect a child may have SPD in the vestibular area, the child should have a thorough vision screening with an optometrist to rule out basic vision problems.

The publisher grants permission for this page to be photocopied for distribution for teacher's classroom use only.
© Gryphon House, Inc. 800.638.0928. www.ghbooks.com

Proprioception Avoider: Red Flags

The Proprioception Avoider may

❖ appear lazy or overly tired;

❖ avoid physical activities (running, jumping, skipping, or hopping);

❖ be a picky eater;

❖ prefer not to move; or

❖ dislike other people moving his or her body (not want you to help him or her place his or her arms into his or her coat).

Proprioception Seeker: Red Flags

The Proprioception Seeker may

❖ enjoy crashing into walls, objects, or people;

❖ bite his or her fingernails or suck his or her thumb or fingers;

❖ demonstrate aggressive behaviors such as hitting, kicking, or biting;

❖ be unaware of other person's personal space (get in your face when he or she is talking or lie on you when you are sitting);

❖ request that you tie his or her shoes very tightly;

❖ stomp his or her feet when walking;

❖ chew on objects, including his or her shirt, pencils, markers, toys, and gum;

❖ like to be patted very firmly or wrapped tightly in a blanket during rest time; or

❖ participate in rough-and-tumble play that is extremely forceful.

Proprioception Under-Responder: Red Flags

The Proprioception Under-Responder may:

❖ not be aware when someone bumps into him or her;

❖ have poor small motor skills (for example, cutting, drawing, writing, feeding);

❖ be slow to learn how to undress/dress self;

❖ be uncoordinated with large motor skills (for example, walking, running, hopping, skipping);

❖ not cry when significant injury occurs;

❖ appear disinterested in movement experiences; or

❖ break toys easily because he or she has difficulty manipulating objects.

Note: If you suspect a child may have SPD in the proprioception area, the child should have a thorough vision screening with an optometrist to rule out basic vision problems.

The publisher grants permission for this page to be photocopied for distribution for teacher's classroom use only.
© Gryphon House, Inc. 800.638.0928. www.ghbooks.com

Index